What people are saying about

Practically Pagan: An Alternative Guide to Planet Friendly Living

A very much needed book in these modern times. Our planet needs us to step up. Mabh Savage gives easy, straightforward advice and suggestions that everyone can use. Practical solutions and magical ways to do our bit. We all need this book, before it is too late to save Mother Earth.

Rachel Patterson, author of *Practically Pagan Cooking*, the *Kitchen Witchcraft* series, and other Witchcraft books.

This is an excellent book that brings care for nature into the heart of nature-based spirituality. It is deeply practical, pragmatic and compassionate, and full of easily used ideas. Mabh demonstrates that working for sustainability is an excellent way to deepen your Paganism and enrich your life. Heartily recommended.

Nimue Brown, author of *Druidry and the Future*, *Spirituality Without Structure*, and co-creator of *Hopeless, Maine*.

Caring for our planet is at the very core of the majority of Pagan beliefs, but in today's world of consumerism and excess, it is often difficult to put these beliefs into practice. In this book, Mabh Savage binds the spiritual with the practical by providing examples of how to make rituals, spellwork, and other Pagan elements more eco-friendly as well as bringing the spiritual into the everyday things we can do to help the planet such as re-cycling and composting.

Dan Coultas, author of *The Gods' Own County: A Heathen Prayer Book* and Community Support Officer for the Pagan Federation.

PRACTICALLY PAGAN

An Alternative Guide to Planet Friendly Living

PRACTICALLY PAGAN

An Alternative Guide to Planet Friendly Living

Mabh Savage

MOON
BOOKS
Winchester, UK
Washington, USA

JOHN HUNT PUBLISHING

First published by Moon Books, 2022
Moon Books is an imprint of John Hunt Publishing Ltd., No. 3 East Street, Alresford
Hampshire SO24 9EE, UK
office@jhpbooks.net
www.johnhuntpublishing.com
www.moon-books.net

For distributor details and how to order please visit the 'Ordering' section on our website.

Text copyright: Mabh Savage 2021

ISBN: 978 1 78904 445 4
978 1 78904 446 1 (ebook)
Library of Congress Control Number: 2020952021

A CIP catalogue record for this book is available from the British Library.

Design: Matthew Greenfield

UK: Printed and bound by CPI Group (UK) Ltd, Croydon, CR0 4YY
Printed in North America by CPI GPS partners

We operate a distinctive and ethical publishing philosophy in
all areas of our business, from our global network of authors to
production and worldwide distribution.

Contents

This book is the culmination of a commitment to An Mórrígan; a promise that my pledge to try and make the world a better place is more than just words; it's words I share with other people, in the understanding of the power of words to give shape to the universe. It's also for Nathan, who looks at the world as something to be cherished and enjoyed in its natural state. So say we all.

About the Author

Mabh Savage is a pagan author and musician with a particular interest in Irish Celtic spirituality. She's also a member of the global Covenant of Hekate and has assisted in some fascinating collaborative projects such as working with members all over the world to create a song for Hekate (Mother of Dreams, available on Mabh's SoundCloud, https://soundcloud.com/mabh-savage).

Mabh is the secretary of the Pagan Federation Children and Families Team which aims to make life easier for Pagan families in Great Britain. She's also the current editor of Aether, the magazine for Pagan families.

She's been a member of the UK Green Party for many years, and believes firmly that it's possible to reverse the damage being done to our planet with the right focus and action now.

www.mabhsavage.com
https://www.patreon.com/MabhSavage
https://www.facebook.com/MabhSavage
https://twitter.com/Mabherick

Previous Books
A Modern Celt ISBN-10: 1780997965
Pagan Portals: Celtic Witchcraft ISBN-10: 1785353144

Acknowledgments

This book wouldn't exist without the support of Moon Books and particularly Trevor Greenfield, so thank you for the chance to write and publish this book on a subject about which I am so passionate, now more than ever.

Heartfelt thanks also go out to Nimue Brown for inspiring me in any number of ways, making me think about my songs for trees again, and, of course, the tireless work in terms of publicity and marketing.

I'm also eternally grateful to Debi Gregory, an upcoming co-author for a future book and the reason I am involved in the Pagan Federation and wider Pagan community. Debi, you have a gift for inspiring others to be better than they are, a gift that I would be proud to have even a small fraction of.

My siblings Kay and Connie, you are both a reminder that the best way to go through this world is to just be yourself as hard as you can and never bow to other folx' expectations. Kay, your work with XR in 2020 was nothing short of heroic, and I never stop thinking about the example you set for your daughter. You showed her and me that you truly can be the change you wish to see in the world.

I'd like to thank Sarah Kerr, president of the Pagan Federation in the UK for the amazing introduction to this book and her tireless work to make the PF a kind, inclusive place to be.

To every member of the Pagan community that answered questions about their practice and which aspects of environmentally friendly living were important to them, I am so grateful for the inspiration you gave me, much of which resides within the chapters of this book.

Finally, to my immediate family: My husband, Jim, who gave me the space and time to finish this book and who is endlessly supportive. My daughter, Ember, who as I write this is a feral toddler who loves every living thing she comes across and long may that continue. My step-son, George, who has a million different ways with kindness. And my son, Nathan, who is perhaps my biggest fan but also my biggest critic, egging me on and keeping me grounded all at the same time. Nathan, your ideas and imagination always inspire me. You worked with me on videos about sustainability and wildlife that inspired others to take action to be kinder in their gardens and homes, so even at ten years old, you're already making a difference. You make me so proud.

This book is for anyone who wonders if they could make a difference. You can.

Foreword

The climate crisis we currently find ourselves living in is without a doubt one of the biggest and most important challenges that we as humans face in the world right now. We need to find ways to balance the lives we live with the way the world works, its available resources and how we manage those. I believe that this issue is something that the majority of Pagans will be united on, given that statistics tell us that over 90% of all people who call themselves Pagan practise a varying range of environmentally sound behaviours such as using public transport over private vehicles, recycling, growing their own produce and buying second-hand clothing. Indeed, I am one of that over 90%.

Everyone knows in one way or another that you can only get people to do things like this if there is some benefit; therefore, there must be a motivating purpose to our practise of environmentalism. I believe the answer is to be found in our faith practices.

As Pagans, we bring together our faith, our morality and environmentalism often, and many are to be found working hard on efforts to help the planet in one way or another. We are largely happy to inconvenience ourselves to help our planet and help others to find the understanding we have about humankind's current abuse of available resources, because we understand the reality of where our collective modern ways of life are leading us. Indeed, we even have a Pagan charity dedicated to helping sustainable nature and society projects (PaganAid). I believe the reasons we contribute in these ways are to be found in our faith too.

Our fundamental shared belief, no matter which individual path we follow, is that the natural world and the life it sustains is sacred. Every single bit of it. Our individual paths have us exploring the world in different ways and observing practises that are personal to us as individuals rather than identical across a whole group of people. We do of course though, share many commonalities.

Most of us recognise that we humans are neither above, nor separate from nature. We are after all mammals - animals with self-awareness and the ability to solve complex problems. Nature encompasses us just as much as it does the seas, the forests, the land and all the life that lives within it.

Being a part of nature means that we live within its tides, too. We understand that nothing can be in a state of constant growth, there is a need for dormancy and rest. We feel the connection between us and every other living thing as if we were all just different branches of the same tree. Thankfully, scientific exploration is now beginning to understand in finer detail that which we have known all along – that the biosphere we call our home is an entire and single ecosystem, each part of it vital to its optimum functioning. Much like our own bodies, or an engine, if one part fails there is an effect on every other part until eventually, if left unattended, the whole thing fails once and for all.

We see our human family much the same. We're all connected to each other through our families. Right back through the ages until the beginning of mankind and beyond to the species we first evolved from, in the same way crocodiles and birds can count dinosaurs as their connected family and the trees and plants that are familiar to us now evolved from other connected species.

Not only are we connected right here, right now but we feel a connection with every living thing that's ever been in existence through our reverence and understanding for nature. A part of our understanding and connection with nature is through working with the elements of the natural world. We understand of course that this is a simplistic model, breaking things down into their most basic of forms of being and seeing them through human rather than scientific eyes. Those elements are air, fire, wind, earth, and spirit. Each living thing, including water, plants, the earth itself, animals, people etc is made up of these basic elements. We are air just as much as the wind, giving food to the trees and plants as we exhale and in return receiving the gift of oxygen from them. We are fire burning the energy of the sun as we eat plants to nourish our bodies and we in turn bring passion to life. We are water with the oceans in our DNA and as we use the same water that nourished all life before us to nourish ourselves. We are earth as we share the same elemental elements as all other life meaning we can be human one day and part of the make-up of a mountain on another. We are spirit when all that comes together as it needs to in order to create flourishing, sustainable life that is interconnected.

We understand to our cores that cutting down our forests is to our planet as smoking is to our own lungs. Mining vital minerals is as devastating to the earth as vitamin or mineral deficiencies are to our health. Polluting our water sources makes as much sense to having a healthy world as drinking nothing but energy drinks does to our bodies.

We as humans largely feel compelled to avoid things that cause harm to our bodies yet collectively, we have been turning a blind eye for the last couple of hundred years to the damage we have been inflicting to our home; the thing that gives us life. If you look closely you can see it everywhere in society too. We are collectively disconnected from nature, living outside of it and trying to control it to our own ends, and this leads to further disconnection within our communities. People stop caring about others, indeed even see them as threats, and so the fabric of society becomes selfish, insular and inward facing.

We know through our reverence and study of the natural world that the answer to all these ills is to create sustainable solutions. It cannot possibly mean that we maintain our current levels of consumption, just as much as our economic and political systems must also change if they are to be a part of building those solutions. We need to build a global connected culture – an ecosystem that is free of domination and exploitation. Imagine if you will, a world of local economies that link together in sustainable ways that are of benefit to all. This will mean overhauling our food systems, our transport systems and distribution of resources, our ways of life even from what we wear to how we think and feel. It will mean an honest and critical assessment of those things humanity truly values and needs to flourish in a healthy world. It will need an army of people who understand the urgency of the problem to carry out the work that needs to be done and they will need to know that most of the human population of the world is on their side.

There are things we can do right now. We need to examine each individual, community and nation's activities when it comes to things that are unsustainable. We are all responsible, as much for ourselves as we are for our countries, because of that connection to everything I spoke about earlier. What happens to the earth, happens to us and happens to our communities.

Technical solutions are presenting themselves. There are amazing people out there who create them in abundance, but unless political will changes, those solutions may never become mainstream and get put into practice. We have a responsibility to show that we want a change in politics from being defined by economic growth to a system based on the health of its population and preservation of its natural environments in order to save our burning house. This will require a collective shift in our most deeply held values around what it means to be human and the responsibilities we have to our caretaking of the world as a part of that. There is nothing that shifts perspectives more than connection and practising of spirituality, and especially when that means finding deeper meaning for ourselves in the natural world extra to our scientific understanding of it. As individuals, we can begin doing that right now simply by getting out of our houses and workplaces and getting out into nature to really explore and find those connections. This will have a knock-on effect on everything else we touch in our lives and so the ripple effect then works its way out to the communities we are personally a part of.

It can't stop there though, and if the collective shift can be made starting with the individual then there is no reason it should. When people build sustainable communities, they then grow a collective voice for change within wider communities.

Fundamentally, due to our understanding and connection with nature and all life, we Pagans believe that a collective change in spirit is what's needed. One that fosters a new relationship between humanity and the natural world, one that our ancestors knew before when they lived by the seasons and the wheel of nature, and we are sure we can know again because we live it each day.

We strive every day in our work, play and daily lives to connect to the harmony of the natural world. The song it sings touches us all the way through to our bones, we feel it in our breath, our thoughts, our bodies and our spiritual nature. We work hard at developing that connection and honouring it with our practices so that we never lose touch with it.

Pagans can be of huge help in our current crisis because of their understanding of the issues around sustainability, and simply by helping others to find their connection to nature in order to help them understand that we cannot continue to be disconnected and held aside from our heritage of being a part of nature. Showing others how to sustain the interconnected web of life, beginning with themselves and their communities, is how we can be useful and affect real change. We commit to using all our knowledge, resources and abilities to foster the change that our world so desperately needs. We offer ourselves in service to working towards an entirely healthy earth that includes all aspects of the life that lives on it.

We want to see the elemental balance returned to the planet and therefore, as individuals, communities and members of the global community we strive to promote the current and future health of our home world in order to create a truly sustainable future for our children and the generations that follow. Indeed, we believe we have no real choice in that. We must either find ways to become sustainable, and quickly, or we die out as a race and make the planet uninhabitable for everything else left behind us.

It can be confusing with the wealth of advice out there to know what you can do to help the effort. *Practically Pagan: An Alternative Guide to Planet Friendly Living* is crammed full of practical ways in which you can help and do your own bit towards solving the issue of the climate crisis so that you can find the ways that suit you and your life best. It's a great way to start on the path to sustainable living as much as it is useful to those who are already making efforts to do their bit. After all, it is our duty to be the change we want to see in the world and we all have to start somewhere.

Sarah Kerr, President of the Pagan Federation UK, 2020

Introduction

First off, I want to be clear that I'm not an academic expert on environmental matters. On that note, whenever I quote statistics or figures, I'm going to cite my sources, and aim to give sources that are as unbiased as possible. There's a lot of misinformation out there when it comes to our amazing planet, but with a bit of digging and some skill with a search engine or at the library, it's possible to figure out fact from fiction.

So, I'm no expert, but I have spent a great deal of my life looking after my small patch of this planet and trying to encourage others to do the same. I used to campaign for the Green Party in my local community, and while I don't think environmental matters should be wholly political (we all live on this planet, after all, regardless of beliefs), it was nice to be able to make a small difference in the community, even if it was watching a local councillor sort out getting some rubbish picked up, or petitioning to stop a green area being built over.

I think it's these local actions that add up to big differences across the world. One of the worst problems we have, I believe, is that folks think they *can't* make a difference. That what they do is too small to count. *Believe me* it makes a difference. Every light you switch off, every time you recycle, every drop of water you save. Because if one person thinks it makes a difference, then that means 100, or 1000, or 1,000,000 could be thinking the same. And that's a whole lot of electricity or water saved, or small green patches that didn't get built over, or garbage that didn't end up in landfill.

How does this tie into paganism? For me, that's pretty simple. I walk a nature based path, and honour the turn of the seasons (in my little corner of the Northern Hemisphere), and understand that humans are not the only lifeform that matters. My deities have been around way before our industrial and technological landscape, and will no doubt linger in some form or other long after we have vanished from this planet. I feel the spirits inside of everything from the trees in my garden to the laptop I'm writing on, and sense that there is truly a connectedness about all things. However, I can only honour that connection if I'm willing to take responsibility for my part in causing damage to it.

It's a harsh truth, perhaps, that so much that humans do, that *we* as individuals or communities do every day, causes damage to our amazing planet. Every car journey, every mobile phone upgrade, and every hot bath – yes, I do think about things to that level of minutiae! But I also believe that humans have a right to exist. We evolved here, and this is our planet. We can earn our place in this world if we just tread a little more carefully. Move, perhaps, a little more gently through this web of wonder that life creates every moment across the planet we call home.

With that in mind, I wanted to create this book as a practical volume that will allow you to assess the way you currently practice your faith, decide if changes need to be made, and discover practical ways to make those changes. I'm not expecting anyone to uproot their lives and suddenly go off-grid, so fear not! That's not the aim of this book. I want to encourage you to be more mindful in your practice, considering the Earth you walk upon, and the impact your faith, spirituality, or religious practice has on the environment around you.

Mabh Savage

Chapter 1

Planet Friendly Paganism

If you're a Pagan, or interested in Pagan spirituality, the chances are you probably already have a great deal of reverence for our beautiful planet. You understand that humans are just one species in a world full of amazing plants and animals, and that just because we are at the top of the food chain that doesn't give us the right to destroy indiscriminately.

Sounds good? Excellent. We are on the same page - figuratively and literally! Living a life that is kind to the world around us can seem difficult at times, but there are many ways in which we can make small changes that amount to big differences. Having a spirituality based in the love of the land and all that walks, crawls or flies above it helps enormously, I find.

Within this book, I may speak about my own path, which is heavily based in Irish Celtic mythology. I'm also a member of the Covenant of Hekate and take Her sacred virtues – compassion, courage, temperance, justice and wisdom – very seriously. However, I hope that everything I speak about in this book can be adopted by anyone regardless of the specifics of your path. I guess what's key is that my Paganism moves me to do more, to do better, and to walk gently upon this planet. For, in the words of Mike Berners-Lee, "there is no Planet B."

As I write this first chapter, I'm sat thinking about the day I had. We live a fairly standard modern life. We have electronic devices, appliances, a fridge freezer and Wi-Fi. We have to buy food from the supermarkets from time to time, so we're certainly not self-sufficient. We use a dryer when we need clothes urgently – there are five of us in our fairly modest house, including three small humans, so there's always a pile of washing waiting to go on! My point is, we're hardly off-grid and we certainly have a carbon footprint. What makes a difference is that we are, as a family, hyper-aware of that. By becoming aware of a problem, you become able to address it and do something about it. And, that's exactly what we try to do and try to inspire others to do.

Today, I tore up kitchen roll and toilet roll inners to add to my compost pile. I tutted my way around the house switching off lights and other devices. I used cold water where I could instead of engaging the gas-powered boiler. I used abandoned glasses of water (why do kids always have at least three drinks scattered around the house?!?) to water the house plants. I made sure the watering cans were angled so they caught the (relentless) rain. I took the slightly soft fruit which no one would eat and prepared it for jam. I also cleaned and sterilised jars from shop-bought foods to use for said jam.

All of this is normal for me. I take these actions in my stride, and rarely think of them as chores. Okay, occasionally I get fed up with the compost bin, especially when we had a ludicrous infestation of fruit flies. Thankfully, the compost bin is in the very top of the back garden far away from the house, so it only affected me personally when I was undoing the compost bin and dealing with the tiny swarm flying at me in indignation.

The position of my compost bin is not accidental. Not only is it carefully placed away from the house, but it's almost directly in the north of the garden, signifying (for some) the element of Earth. Earth can mean many things but at its most literal it is the land we walk upon, the soil, the creatures who benefit from that; grains of sand, massive mountains, rocks, rubble, gravel... and everything connected to those things. Every time I tip a bowl of potato peelings and teabags into my compost bin, I feel like I'm giving an offering back to the Earth, this amazing planet that gives us life, sustenance and wonder. Sometimes I murmur a prayer of gratitude, perhaps for the food I enjoyed ahead of my trip to the compost bin. Perhaps to a deity I am performing work for. Perhaps simply to the Earth.

There's more about the magic of daily activities in greater detail later in this book, but this is just one clear example of where my paganism directly influences my relationship with this daily task. This spiritual connection, in turn, makes the task seem much less like a chore and more like an act of worship. Even the fruit flies, pesky though they seem, live because of my acts and my motivation to reduce waste and landfill. I hold my breath to avoid them flying in my mouth, but I'm grateful for their existence and understand their place in the ecosystem.

Another way in which my Paganism is tied to my desire to make the world a better place is in the offerings I leave on my altar. As much as possible, I use organic offerings that can later be buried, composted, or left for other lifeforms to enjoy. A good example is a loaf of devotional bread I made for the Morrigan recently. I used a grain called Einkorn which is classed as an ancient grain, so old it was found in the stomach of Ötzi the Iceman, thought to be at least 5,300 years old (Maixner, 2018). The bread was made without shop-bought yeast, using natural yeasts from the flour and the environment to make a sourdough. The finished bread was dense but tasty, a rich and dark loaf which went astonishingly well with a local goat's milk cheese. My mouth is watering simply recalling this! Some of the bread went for offerings on my Morrigan altar. Once She was done with it, I left it on my bird feeder safe in the knowledge that both my Goddess and the natural world would benefit from this.

As you read this, perhaps you can think of ways that you regularly show kindness to the planet. Maybe you take regular trips to your recycling centre. Maybe you have a space for growing food, flowers, or herbs. Perhaps you are a talented upcycler, crafting amazing things out of resources others might simply throw out.

Action: Take a pen and paper or a digital device with a notebook app. Think of all the ways you already help the planet. Be as detailed or as abstract as you like. If you have nothing, fear not, this book will help you with that. If you have plenty, that's amazing and you should be proud. The same goes if you have even one action on your list. Try and think about how any of these actions link into your spirituality or the sense of how you connect with this world. Try and put it into words. If you struggle to write, use a voice recorder or even paint or draw how this makes you feel.

Throughout this book you'll find actions or tasks that you can perform to help you get more out of this volume. However, they're obviously not mandatory and if you pick this book up even occasionally as a reminder of why it's good to be kind to our planet, well, that's delightful to me. Sometimes, it seems there's an apathy throughout the Western world when it comes to caring for the Earth. A sense that no matter what, things will be okay. This false positivity covers the very real threats of climate change, pollution, loss of habitat for wildlife, the extinction of species, and the rapid depletion of natural resources. Don't worry – I'm not expecting you, dear reader, to fix any of these problems on your own. But, imagine if we all worked together to do our bit. What a difference we could make then.

If you've written about or even thought about your current impact on the world around you, then it's time to move forward with this volume. During the next few chapters, we'll work together on making small changes that carry a surprisingly big impact, updating altars and sacred spaces, and working with ritual both indoors and outdoors for minimal environmental impact. Ready?

Chapter 2

The New 3 Rs: Reduce, Reuse, Recycle

If you're not old enough to remember being taught the "Three Rs" in school, then count yourself lucky! This stems from a time when education was all about Reading, W(r)iting and A(r)ithmetic to the tragic exclusion of pretty much anything else. Let's face it, what good does it do to teach our kids about 'rithmetic there isn't a decent planet to use it in? I firmly believe that the next generation is our best hope for a cleaner, more whole planet, and that starts with guidance from us. I think the best way to give that sort of guidance is by living that experience and becoming wiser about it ourselves.

Reducing, reusing, and recycling are three ways of dealing with rubbish: refuse, garbage, trash, waste. There's no getting away from it. As humans, we make a whole lot of it. And we're not the only beings to do it. It's just that because of this industrial and technological society and civilization, ours tends to be a bit more toxic than, say, a fox's rotten food remnants, or the many pellets of owls. We've introduced to this world the concept of wasting things that aren't organic. Things that take a long time to biodegrade, or that release toxins as they do. However, throwing things away isn't optional. We cannot live in piles of our own waste. One of the first steps in becoming mindful or spiritual about our rubbish is to forge a spiritual connection to the things we get rid of.

Letting Go Responsibly and Spiritually

Letting go of clutter and rubbish is an essential part of life, and unavoidable. As a Pagan, you may feel guilty for the amount of stuff you throw away, but you can turn waste disposal into a spiritual experience by following one or more of the following tips.

Only throw away what you have to. Don't hoard unnecessarily, but avoid "single-use" items and try and find a way to reuse stuff rather than chucking it out.

Recycle as much as you can. Thankfully, most homes are now part of areas where councils or local government offices run regular recycling pick-ups. When I was a child, we had one, small, black, metal bin which the bin crew would collect weekly. Nowadays, we have three huge wheelie bins: one for garden waste, one for recyclables and one for everything else. Make sure you understand what can go in your recycling bin. If you don't have one, check with your local waste processing centre what you can drop off with them.

Have you got a garden with space for a compost bin? Composting is a wonderful way to create your own soil additives and it also has the spiritual aspect of giving back to the earth and avoiding waste. Add waste vegetables, fruits, garden clippings, eggshells, coffee grounds and even some types of wastepaper to your compost bin. Add discarded items from your altars or sacred spaces if appropriate- do not compost anything you have promised away, for example, I would never compost garlic I had left as an offering on Hekate's altar. This is normally buried at a crossroads or carefully potted if it has already started to grow unaided. Flowers from a Spring Equinox display could go in the compost, or perhaps be left under a sacred plant in the garden. Follow the guidelines of your own path and your own instincts.

Give to charity. Old clothes that don't fit anymore can often be used by someone else. Charity shops and clothes recycling services always need donations.

Share with your community. Before something goes in the bin, ask your friends, family, neighbours and spiritual community if they can use it. I've passed incense, crystals, books (so many books!) and even altar decorations on in this way. Just because they weren't right for me anymore doesn't mean someone else won't enjoy them. I've also received beautiful divination cards and artwork in the same way. If you have ensouled a piece of artwork or statue, or imbued an item with a great deal of energy, consider reversing this (if possible) before giving it away. Seek advice from a spiritual, religious or magical elder or mentor.

Dispose mindfully. When you give something away or throw it away, thank it for its presence in your life. Feel the gratitude for the impact it has had. If it's something you hate, feel gratitude for this prompting you to remove it from your home! Gratitude is a healing feeling and filling yourself with it as you declutter can make the process much more rewarding.

Action: How do you feel about letting go of things you have little use for? Does it pass by without comment? Are you connected to the things that leave your life? Are you a hoarder? We all deal with "stuff" differently; there are no right or wrong answers. Make a list of the things you have thrown away recently, and how it made you feel. Now list three things you think you should get rid of, and why. Let these thoughts run without judgement. Now think about how you might dispose of these things mindfully, with as little environmental impact as possible. Does this make you feel better about getting rid of them? Are you considering keeping one of them now? Or does it make you feel more at peace with their release? This exercise is about exploring your relationship to your things; your physical belongings.

Please don't feel that you are "wrong" in some way for hanging onto things, or for throwing too much away. We are all different. We all have different size homes and storage options. Different things have different levels of significance to each of us. Be wary of folks who say, "You should get rid of that". Only *you* can say what should or shouldn't be in your life.

Recycling

Most places in the developed world now provide facilities which make it easier to recycle. If your local authority does not provide this, you could consider campaigning for it to be introduced – see Chapter 10 for more making a difference within the community. If they aren't swayed by the many environmental benefits, they might be swayed by the financial aspects. Every tonne of landfill is taxed by national government. Landfills owned by private companies charge to use their facilities, as do incineration companies. Plus, improving recycling facilities increases jobs, adding to the economy (Katy Wheeler, University of Essex, 2019), so really, why wouldn't local authorities want to help you recycle?

If recycling is not collected from your home or street, check if there's an accessible waste management site nearby. We have a local, council run site which has, in recent years, transformed from "rubbish tip" to a full-blown recycling centre. They accept clothes, batteries, old tins of paint, appliances, furniture, plus a whole host of plastics, metals and paper products. You have to have a pass to show that you're a local resident, and you have to book a slot as it can get busy! A good sign, perhaps, that more people are using the facility now than ever.

Why is recycling so important? British households produce between 23 and 26 million tonnes of waste every year (DEFRA, 2020). Yet only 43.5% of that is recycled. In the U.S, things are even more dire. Only 21.4% of waste is recycled, with not-for-profit organisations like Recycle Across America citing public confusion around what can and can't be recycled as a top factor in this. Understanding what can go in your recycling bin is crucial, as if a recycling bin or container is contaminated, sometimes refuse collectors will move the whole lot to landfill.

Other positive benefits of recycling include cleaner air, protection of natural resources, and as mentioned before, the creation of jobs and opportunities within industries that work towards a greener future. According to Recycle Across America, if the U.S alone could hit a 75% recycling target, it would be the equivalent of removing 55 million cars from the roads thanks to the reduction in CO2 emissions. Quite astonishing.

Recycling also protect our waterways and water supplies. Drilling and mining for the natural resources needed to make plastics, metal products and more uses vast amounts of water: 1% of global water usage is taken up by mining, at around 4,000 million gallons of water per day (USGS, 2015). Can you even imagine what that much water looks like? I'm not sure I can!

Recycling helps prevent plastic ending up in the ocean, a problem that cannot be overstated. I've covered this in greater detail in the next chapter, that our blasé attitudes as a society that have, for so long, placed convenience over kindness to our world, have to change.

Pagan Recycling Opportunities
Always check your local facilities to confirm what materials they do and do not accept for recycling.

- Tealight cases: tealights are the smaller candles that have individual cases, so they instantly come with a waste factor. However, they are very useful and help avoid having to use drippy candles that can cause damage. The cases are usually metal or plastic, and both are widely recyclable.
- Damaged wands, staves, or staffs: It's very sad when a beloved wooden tool becomes damaged or broken. If they really can't be fixed, or cut down to make other tools, then they may be composted or recycled. Check with your local recycling pick up if they accepts chunks of wood. I know ours will accept what they class as "small branches" but if we have anything truly robust, we have to take it to the recycling centre ourselves. Another option here is to mulch it and use it on your garden, or even to burn it. Many folks use wood-fired heating or multi-fuel stoves. It's better to replenish your fuel stores for free rather than

your sacred tool ending up in landfill! As always, if a tool is dedicated to a particular deity or spirit, check via your connection to them if any of these actions are appropriate.

- Spell sheets, written work, study papers etc: If you don't need to keep something for future reference or follow up work, or you have it digitally, make sure all paper goes in your recycling unless you plan to burn or bury it ritually.
- Leftover incense: If the incense has burned right down to ash, simply compost it. Ash of all kinds is beneficial for compost, as it can balance out the acidity caused by decomposition. Try not to throw chunks of unburned charcoal into your compost, as they sometimes contain additives which can be harmful to some plants. If you know your charcoal is additive free, that's okay! If incense is only partially burned, you can simply use it again.
- Offerings: I always try and use offerings that I can safely dispose of without having to use my local refuse facilities – more on this in detail in Chapter 4. Most organic offerings can be composted, if that is appropriate to you and your sacred connections. Others could be perhaps given to wildlife, for example, I may use almonds as an offering to Hekate, but once they have past their usefulness as an offering, I will move them outside for the birds and squirrels. I'm reliably informed that Hekate is okay with this! Depending on the time of the month and the purpose of my offering, I may leave them at the point in my garden that most resembles a crossroads, a sacred place for Hekate. Offerings of alcohol or sugary things like chocolate may have to be disposed of more carefully. Some local authorities now have the facility to take food waste for mass composting. Or, you may be permitted by your path to recycle the offerings into something else: chocolate into a chocolate cake, perhaps, that you could then use again as offerings. Or simply enjoy!

Reduce

Reducing the use of resources simply means buying or taking only what we need. In my old coven, we used to have a mantra during our offerings section of ritual, which was, "Take only what we can reasonably expect to put back." That's really stuck with me throughout my continued learning, and I try and live by that sentiment as much as possible.

At its most basic, it means buying only what you need, or in broader terms, *taking* only what you need. You may be a forager, picking elderberries in autumn, but you know to leave some for the birds. If we strip the tree, not only is there none for anyone or anything else, but the tree itself can't reproduce. There is a spiritual significance in understanding what we need now, what we should store for the future, and what we can do without.

Having said that, I'm certainly not promoting a terribly frugal or spartan lifestyle. Life is short and small pleasures should be enjoyed whenever the opportunity arises. If that small pleasure is indulging in yet another deck of tarot cards (you know who you are!), a new set of runes, or a favourite incense you just can't live without, then you should be able to do these things without feeling guilty.

The key is to find a balance between having the things that make you happy and fulfil you in some way, and looking after the world by reducing the resources used and emissions produced to create and ship new things. Ask yourself three things:

- Do you really need it?
- Do you really want it?
- Can you live, joyfully, without it?

If you answer "Yes" to the first one, you can ignore the other two. If you answer "Yes" to the second once, then have it, you deserve nice things! If you answer "Yes" to the third one, then it's probably okay to leave it in the shop or on the website on this occasion.

Another way to reduce your reliance on store-bought items is to learn how to make your own pagan or spiritual resources. Chapter 5 has a few simple ideas for incense ingredients, and other things that can be simple to make at home and that you can do with very basic, easily available and low environmental-impact ingredients.

Re-use

Re-using an item is *by far* the most environmentally friendly way to go about dealing with the things that are no longer useful in their current form or situation. Recycling is great but still uses some energy and water, so finding a new and inventive use for old things protects our planet even further.

I was given a beautiful willow stave once. My tribe and I had built a small lodge together at a modern sacred site, with permission, and undertaken a spiritual weekend of reflection and community. Once we had done, we returned the land to its original state, removing the bendy willow used to build the lodge. Some of the staves were planted, and as willow tends to, quickly rooted and became a natural fence for another part of the site. My shaft of willow was a bit older and dryer, but a little too tall for a staff – it towered over me! I carefully sawed off the top of the pole, and suddenly had a bit of spare willow wood that had no use. Instead of throwing it away, though, I decided to make a matching wand to go with my staff. I polished and carved the wood, treating it first with linseed oil and then with natural beeswax. It gave me joy, not just because I'd made a beautiful pair of tools I was proud of, but because I'd avoided having to dispose of a part of an experience that meant so much to me.

Upcycling is a fairly new term, and one I love. It means taking something that you no longer need in its current function, and using it to make something you do need, or perhaps simply want. Some of my favourite Pagan upcycling projects include:

- Using items like sea glass or pebbles with wire or disused leather thong to make jewellery.
- Using old, worn clothes to make new ones, such as ritual wear or warm outer layers for woodland journeys or similar.
- Turning worn or rusted incense holders into containers for other items, like non-liquid offerings or altar decorations.
- Old tins or boxes into portable altars – what would you have in yours? I am thinking of creating one with a tealight, a lighter, a shell, and three equal sized and shaped but differently coloured pebbles in for simple divination, a technique I learned at the Irish Pagan School.
- Rebind old, battered notebooks to use as journals, spell books, or dream diaries.
- Leftover candle wax can be melted down and used to make new candles, or for other purposes such as waterproofing something. I once used the very end of an altar candle to make a decorative stamp in the back of a book that was filled with my learnings for that year.

Any fabric can be cut, stitched and decorated to make an altar cloth or wall hanging. We have a "rag bag" in our house, and any time someone outgrows or wears out something that can't be passed along to someone, it goes in there. These bits of clothing come out from time to time to be tortured by my poor sewing skills! It's not my forte, but I've made a few items like microwaveable rice bags (for fellow witches with bad backs) and small pouches for stones or incense.

Leaves, seeds, flowers and other natural offerings can often be dried and kept. I save flower heads and dry them out to use as pot pourri. Me and my ten-year-old have made garlands out of autumn leaves, and one of our proudest projects is a season tree which lives in the front hallway. It's a large, branched twig he found, plus a variety of items from my altars and from use within ritual. These include colourful autumn leaves, evergreen leaves like ivy, feathers, seeds and more.

Autumn leaves can also be fixed to glass or transparent plastic with clear PVA glue, making incredible seasonal decorations such as a maple leaf candle holder. Press the leaf against the glass while it's still slightly soft; if you wait until it's dry and crisp it will simply shatter when you try this. Brush PVA glue over the leaf. Wait a few seconds then add another layer. Repeat until the leaf has no chance of peeling away from the glass. Note: PVA is a synthetic polymer and will release toxic fumes if burned, so only ever have it on the outside of candle holders and never where the flame can touch it! PVA a product of the petrochemical industry, so for an even more eco-friendly option, source your own glue or try making your own in small batches for minimal waste.

Action: Have you ever repurposed or upcycled something in your spiritual path? What was it? What was the difference in the two functions? Were they connected? Take a look at the items you use in your everyday life, particularly connected to your faith or spirituality. Is there something you were thinking of getting rid of? Could you find another use for it, or change it in some way to become useful again?

Chapter 3

Elements

Elements are an important part of many Pagan paths. If you don't particularly subscribe to the Western elemental concepts of Earth, Air, Fire and Water, or similar groupings such as Earth, Sea and Sky, you may still find ways in the following chapters to honour the cradles of these concepts: the earth beneath our feet, the air we breathe, the sun and the power in our homes, and our oceans and waterways.

Earth

The smell of the spring
Is a wondrous thing
Air simply alive
With bacteria sporing
That warm rainy smell
That's the time you can tell
That the wheel has now turned;
On the flip side we dwell.
Day outlives night
The warm golden light
Gives way to the stars
And the nocturnal sight
Of the moon and the owl
And the fox on the prowl
And the cats start to sing
As the dogs start to howl
That the earth is alive
From the snow we survive
Green and strong, we belong
To this world -and we thrive!

Dig my toes in the mud
Plant myself if I could
To be part of the web
Of life, stone, sap and wood.

When we think about environmentally friendly spirituality, the Earth is often the first thing that comes to mind. After all, this aspect of our work is primarily about protecting the planet we walk on: the rocks, the mountains, the plains, the deserts, even the freezing Arctic wastes. The Earth is our home, and as an element, is it any wonder we often associate it with steadfastness, courage, and a warm and loving hearth?

The Earth is, in a way, the primary element. Fire grows within the earth, in the core and in the hearts of volcanoes. Air flows through every tree, around every hill, and into every person's lungs. Water covers around 71% of the surface of the planet, in oceans, rivers, lakes, streams, even those tiny springs that pop out of the side of grassy hills, just waiting to be discovered by thirsty hikers. Earth is the home to all of these, and understanding this helps to see how all the elements, or aspects of our planet, are intrinsically linked and work together to create a world that is uniquely suitable for life. Our use of fire (power and fuels), water, and how we treat the air around us directly impacts the Earth and everything on it.

Despite knowing how deeply intertwined elements are, we love to separate things and honour them separately. Earth often becomes the direction of north, the colours brown or black or green, animals like the bear or the owl, or entities like the great oak tree. For sacred spaces, Earth can be represented by stones, crystals, salt, or icons and symbols that speak to us of our own personal connection to the planet we walk on. Consider adjusting the way you honour Earth with the following environmentally kind tips:

- Use natural altar decorations you have found yourself; more on this in the chapter on Sacred Space.
- If you do take objects from the wild, for example the woods or seashore, make sure it isn't a home for someone. I once picked up a shell out of the surf, and tiny claws poked out around the edges and out popped a very disgruntled hermit crab! Even rocks can have a multitude of life living beneath them.
- Salt is a fine symbol for earth, and is also used in protection, sacred circles, and any number of other spiritual purposes. However, salt can be harmful to plants and some animals, so disposing of it becomes somewhat problematic. If the salt is in a container and hasn't been contaminated (e.g., with oils, incenses) you could donate it if your spiritual practice approves of this. You may also be permitted in your practice to consume the salt yourself. Some waste management sites have facilities to deal with salt. You can save it and use it for salting a pathway or driveway to make it safe in icy weather. Or you could have the same salt that you always use for ritual purposes. Keep this in an airtight container away from moisture to ensure longevity.
- If you use paper in your practice, make sure it is recycled or recyclable. If you plan to burn paper, a common practice for some types of spell work, consider what you will do with the ashes. Ash makes a great addition to compost. If I were petitioning Hekate, I might leave the ashes scattered across the roots of a tree at a crossroads.
- Statuary: Statues, figures, and icons are common across most spiritual and religious paths that I know of. If you can, support a local artist rather than purchasing something mass-produced. Consider the materials the statue is made of: are they ethically sourced and sustainable? How sturdy is it? This is a serious consideration for me,

in a house with three cats and three kids! I don't have the skills to repair a smashed statue and wouldn't purchase something I have to replace a week later.

Incense is a link between Earth and air, using earthly ingredients to create smoke that rises into our olfactory senses and affects us in some way. Check what's in your incense, where it comes from, and another point I look for is to make sure it's not accidentally appropriating the practices of a culture I have no right to. For example, I would never do a smoke-cleansing with white sage. I've heard the opinions of some indigenous folks who are very uncomfortable with this practice becoming widespread. Some tribes weren't allowed to practice smudging until 1978, as it was considered illegal. I'd like to respect that. You may have connections which make the use of white sage perfectly appropriate for you. I respect that too. I tend to smoke-cleanse with rosemary, which I have a strong, personal connection to, and which is a powerful boost to memory. My memory needs all the help it can get!

Look for ways to give back to the Earth, such as planting trees, volunteering with a charity such as the Woodland Trust, or get involved with community initiatives to plant more flowers or start an allotment.

Developing a connection to the Earth can be as simple as pausing each day to breathe and make a note of the feeling of the ground beneath you if you can, or simply visualising it, always moving, spinning, with us bound to it by gravity. I also like to take notice of what's growing outside, which helps me keep track of the seasons. Seeing snowdrops at Imbolc, fresh green birch leaves at Beltane, or salsify seeding at Lughnasadh; these are just some of the things that remind me of my connection to the world around me. I remember that I am a part of nature itself and need to walk gently for my own benefit, just as much as the benefit of the Earth.

Air

I realised I was air today
After years of toying with fire
Getting fingers burned yet
Revelling in the pain
Believing I may be a green witch
A child of the earth
Because I could grow things
Back from almost nothing
Nurturing and coaxing straggling shoots
Back to life.
Then when the house nearly flooded
Over and over
I thought water was mad at me
For not taking notice
For not paying it enough attention
Or respect.
But I realised I was air today.
Standing in the kitchen
The door slightly open
So the cats could run in and out
As they pleased
The wind blew hard and sudden
Trees whipping wildly
And the grass transformed to waves
I felt it
Right down my spine
The thrill of the wind
And I remembered
Laughing on the edge of a cliff
Stormy nights and days made dark to match
Clouds scudding across the moon
Battering door frames and windows
And the slow, elegant breaths of meditation.

Suddenly the rain started
The green garden glinted gloriously
Like a great flat emerald
And the central heating roaring behind me
The fire in my heart and hearth
Of this modern age
And I became confused
With the heat, the soil, the dripping sky
But then the wind howled, triumphant
Clearing the cobwebs away
You are air, they say
Realise, you are air.

I wrote this poem very recently, after realising I identified with the certain aspects of air more closely than any of the other classical Western elements. As the poem states, I still feel my connection to the others, and indeed, the fact that each is an important part of our world and our life. But the feel of the wind on my face or seeing it rip through trees in an alarming way stirs my soul in a particular way. There's unknowable power, that can't truly be seen, but can be felt in any number of ways – just like our deities or spirits. And like them, it can be both giving and destructive.

Storms are an ideal example of this. There have been some terrible storms over the past few years, named deceptively innocuous things like Irma, Harvey and Dennis. Of course, the damage they do is far from innocuous. And climate change is only making things worse. Japanese academics reviewed North Atlantic hurricanes between the years 1968 and 2018. They discovered that the time it takes for a storm to decay has doubled during that 50-year span. That increase is directly linked to warmer seas, so if our oceans continue to warm, we can expect even more dramatic and destructive storms in the decades to come.

As environmentally kind pagans, we can think of the work we do as a way of calming the air, of soothing the temper of the winds, the storms, the hurricanes and their associated beings. We also need to remember that the air is a very significant part of our lives, which we can't help but realise every time we pause to take note of our breath. Many mindfulness practices are based on visualising breathing in positive energy, and breathing out stress or negative feelings. The air is truly like this; we breathe in life giving oxygen, and breathe out carbon dioxide, which in turn is breathed in by the plants around us, who breathe out the oxygen we need. That cycle continues as long as we honour the plants, and don't pollute the air unnecessarily.

Some ways you can adjust your practice to honour the air around you:

- Make sure your incense, candles, and fragrance oils are toxin free.
- Going to a pagan gathering or convention, or a spiritual retreat? Can you car share? The fewer cars on the road, the better. I'm not saying ditch the car completely. I am very personally aware that for some people, cars or other forms of transport are absolutely essential. But if you can share, it makes a real difference in terms of air pollution.
- Symbols of air include feathers, insects or parts of insect, for example butterfly wings. If you use any of these, ensure they are ethically sourced. I only use feathers I have found myself, usually dropped by preening birds.
- Air pollution is caused by a variety of things including fossil fuels, mining, spraying from chemical fertilisers, pesticides, and even volatile organic compounds (VOCs). This last one is gasses emitted from various things we use in our homes such as paint, insect repellents, wood-treatments, and even the plastic packaging on some parcels. This indoor air pollution can cause irritation of

the airways or nausea, and the long-term effects aren't really well understood as yet. Whatever you buy as part of your Pagan or spiritual practice, try and avoid products that contribute to worsening air quality.

- Learn about the creatures of the air: birds, insects, bats, and any esoteric beings you may associated with this ethereal element. Over the past few years, I have developed a relationship with birds that expanded upon a childhood fascination for watching them. I've learned which birds live, nest, or hunt in my local area. I've learned about what gods or pantheons they are associated with. I've found folklore snippets and superstitions. I've written about them, or drawn them (badly!). Gaining a greater understanding of something that lives a large part of its life in this element can really connect you to it in a way you may not have previously thought possible.
- Work with your breath. Find a way that works for you of feeling the breath moving in and out of your body, and forge a connection to the air that fills you then leaves again. The stronger that connection is, the deeper the realisation is that it is something to be honoured and protected.

One of the forms of journeying I do calls to simply breathe, be still and breathe however feel natural. At other times, I follow a pattern of breathing in for five seconds, then out for seven seconds, which is much more structured but I find it can help when I need to manage my anxiety, or simply take a moment to fill my mind with a task to do. The breath is a powerful tool. It literally keeps you alive, but working with it can take you to other realms within your brain, or perhaps outside our physical plane. Clean, safe air has to be a priority, always.

Fire

She gave me a gem
A round cut diamond
Yet oddly purple
In the light from her torches
How did she hold
Two searing fires
Yet stretch out her palm
To show the waiting gift
I knew she handed me
My heart
And though I took it
Grateful and surprised
I now know not what
To do with it.

Fire is an important tool – perhaps the most important. There are numerous myths and legends throughout human history of fire being gifted to humans, and of that being a major turning point in civilization. Imagine our lives before fire: no heat but what we share with our bodies; no cooking; limited choice in medicine; no smelting, smithing, or industry of any kind.

Prometheus is perhaps the most famous bringer of fire. This Greek Titan and creator gifted or restored fire to humanity, depending upon the version of the myth. Prometheus was harshly punished by King of the Greek gods, Zeus, showing the importance of what he had done. The arrival of fire is also linked to Pandora's Box (actually a big earthenware jar), the bringing of sorrow and plague. Perhaps this is an analogy for the fact that progress comes with risk, something we see daily in our world today: the more we advance, the more damage we cause to our beautiful world, and the more we put ourselves at risk of disaster, disease, and destruction.

It's worth noting that the poet Hesiod created Pandora as a

misogynistic "woman is the source of all evil" trope, but truly Zeus was the instigator, setting poor Pandora up as a scapegoat for the woes of humanity: a symbol for abusive patriarchal power if ever there was one.

Prometheus wasn't the only supernatural being who decided that humans deserved fire. In Algonquin myth, the mischief-maker Rabbit stole fire from the Sky People. The fire was passed from creature to creature, curling Squirrel's tail, blackening Crow's feathers, shortening Deer's tail, and eventually hiding in the wood of the trees, where it lives to this day.

The Lenin Lenape Tribe fire story also has a crow in it, the hero of the tale. The crow is a many-hued bird: A Rainbow Crow. The Earth had become cold, too cold for the animals, and they began to fear they would die. Rainbow Crow was chosen to fly to Kijiamuh Ka'ong, the Creator Who Creates By Thinking What Will Be. Rainbow Crow sang a beautiful song and begged the Creator to unthink snow. The Creator, instead, decided to think a new thing: Fire. Rainbow Crow had to fly back to Earth with the fire, and it turned him black and ruined his amazing voice. That is why, to this day, crows are black and croak, but the glossiness and occasional burst of iridescence in their feathers reminds us of the great sacrifice they made for the planet.

Fire keeps us warm; it helps us cook, and it burns the fuels that fire our industries. It is because of fire that we have chemistry, and medicine, and any number of household items. Fire in the home exists in the form of gas power, or electricity, or even candles. Fire is also metaphorical: passion, love, creation, and even anger.

My poem above is called *Dadouchos*, Greek for Torch Bearer. It's one of the epithets of Hekate, an important Goddess in my life and Pagan path. Her fires are literal: she carries twin torches, one in each hand, and they shine like beacons in the darkness. For me, they also represent the twin lights of our eyes, how we see things, our sense of perception – not just literal, but metaphysical. They are the lights of understanding and, every time we reach a crossroads in our lives and need to make a crucial decision, it is those twin torches of intelligence and wisdom that help to keep us moving.

Working with fire in an environmentally mindful way is about respecting its power, its uses, and its alternatives. Never burn fires where they can cause damage to the outdoors, including woodlands, wildlife habitats, or other people's homes or gardens. If you don't know how to build a fire properly, don't attempt to do so without guidance from someone who is experienced. It's a very worthwhile skill to learn! If you have a fire at a camp or gathering, make rules about what can be thrown on it. Don't burn plastics or fabrics, as the resulting smoke can be toxic.

At one of the camps I attend, a central fire is classed as sacred and people are only allowed to burn organic offerings on it e.g. a small corn dolly made out of local grass, or a piece of paper with writing on it. This helps make the practice of protecting the local environment more mindful and sacred.

Choose to do an outdoor ritual at dusk rather than full darkness (if appropriate) to avoid the need for electric lights. Wind up torches or solar powered lamps are also great alternatives to battery powered or plug-in lights. Any batteries used should be rechargeable where possible to avoid waste. As a sidenote, it's not very kind to the local wildlife to suddenly light up a section of their habitat in the middle of the night. For diurnal animals, it disrupts their sleep cycles, and for nocturnal animals, it could ruin their chances of finding a good meal. Fit in with the cycle of the place you are as much as you can.

If you use candles in your practice, find out a little about who is making your candles. Are the candle holders recyclable? Are they made ethically? Do they last? Are the fragrances (if you use them) non-toxic? Most companies are fairly transparent about these aspects of their production process nowadays, so if you can't find a candle supplier that doesn't follow these guidelines, it might be time to switch. Alternatively, you could try making your own candles, which I'll touch on a little more in the chapter on Self-Sufficiency.

Water

Waiting by the ocean
Waiting by the shore
Clouds are hanging, cloaking
Sunlight, grey and raw.
Beach lies glinting wetly
Tide breaks like a sigh
Pebbles crackling, crunching
'Neath the slate tile sky
Winkles, whelks and starfish
Rays and sprays and gulls
Bladderwrack and mermaids purse
Crannies, nooks and pools.
Take me to the ocean
Take me to the shore
Where earth meets sea meets sky
I couldn't ask for more.

Water is life. We cannot live without it. Yet sometimes it's the aspect of our world that we are most thoughtless towards. Some of this comes, perhaps, from much of the Western world having such easy access to water. Turn a tap, there it is. Ta da! Magic water. And you know what, it's okay to revel in the fact that we have water like this. As long as we don't abuse it.

Unfortunately, rather than being amazed every day at just how easy it is for us to access clean, safe water, we seem to have taken it for granted for many years. One aspect of this is seen in how much garbage ends up in our oceans. The Great Pacific garbage patch is one of the worst examples of this. Thankfully, there are many initiatives in place today working towards reducing the amount of pollution in our oceans, plus awareness of the problem has been enhanced by a few ambassadors for our planet, such as the incomparable Sir David Attenborough. His documentary series, Blue Planet 2, raised awareness of the plastic pollution problem perhaps like nothing else this century so far. Since then, plastic bags have been banned in many places or are now chargeable, as have single-use plastic items such as some types of straws and plastic plates and cups. It's worth noting that some folks need to use plastic straws because of disabilities, so we have to be careful to take issues like that into account. But the reduction of single-use plastic is a welcome step in the right direction, as long as we do it mindfully and with as much care for our fellow humans as for the planet.

I began a serious course of elemental work with water around 12 years ago, and it was one of the most refreshing and invigorating spiritual practices I have ever undertaken. Through it I learned about how water is connected to change and transformation, healing, tranquillity, yet also destruction and inevitability. Water isn't the same as air in that it doesn't surround everything. Some places are almost completely dry and rarely see even a drop of rain, like the deserts. Other places are prone to floods and the damage caused by them. Water requires balance, often a recurring theme within many forms of spirituality. Ways to use water in your practice more mindfully include:

- Reuse water where you can. Take water from altars and use it to water plants. You could even have a particular plant dedicated to your practice, a deity, or an aspect of your life you need to serve with honour.
- Some ritual practices call for living water, which is water gathers from natural water sources or rainwater. I sometimes gather rainwater in containers in my garden. Because it's often windy when it rains, these containers

sometimes get leaves and other detritus in. Putting some sort of mesh or open-weave fabric over the container can help with this.

- Consider the different water sources around you. If you don't know, pull up a map of your local area and take a look. You might be surprised by local becks, streams, even natural springs. If you can, get out and explore these waterways, and see the life that forms around them. You could take a small flask or bottle and take some water back with you, as long as you're not disrupting local wildlife. Note: Don't drink water from local waterways unless you have a reliable person tell you it is safe. Bacteria and other problematic organisms can make you very sick.

- If you perform magic or ritual by waterways, never dispose of anything in the water that wasn't there to start with. You can use materials you find around you. For example, making a charm out of driftwood and shells and letting it float away back into the ocean should be fine. Likewise, a tiny poppet made of local reeds or fallen twigs from river-side trees shouldn't cause any harm. Keep offerings small, even if they are organic, to avoid disrupting the local ecosystem.

Being kind to water is also about being kind to yourself. Self-care is a phrase thrown about a lot these days, and it can mean many things to many people. But at its most basic, it's about doing the essential things to keep yourself functioning at a level that works for you.

You are mostly water: stay hydrated. Sleep, and if you can't sleep, seek help, whether that's from a doctor, an ASMR video, or a mindfulness app. Eat well, and be aware that this means different things to different people. Body shape and food are rarely related, so diet or fast only ever because you want to or because it's a safe and desired part of your spiritual practice.

Take pleasure where you can, whether this is in the comfort of others or the beauty of solitude. Rest, whatever this means to you: doing nothing, throwing yourself into your work, or simply being with friends or family. Whatever refills your vessel, do it as regularly as you need to.

Action: What elements resonate with you on your spiritual path? Do you have a particular connection to one more than another? Take some time to think about different elements, and these may be others than I have written here. For example, the elements of Chinese astrology are wood, fire, earth, metal, and water. Some druidic traditions look to the earth, sea and sky, and may see these more as aspects of our existence rather than elements. You may see your path in terms of matter or energy. Write down which elements or universal aspects matter to you, then one way you can change something in your spiritual path related to each one, to make your path more environmentally kind.

For example, I started collecting water from a nearby stream for some ritual purposes rather than using tap water. I can't always do this, as I suffer from hypermobility syndrome and can't always make the walk down, but I hope that the few times I do makes a small difference. What small differences can you make?

Chapter 4

Sacred Space

I know not every reader will have or use an altar or shrine, hence me carefully titling this chapter *Sacred Space* as, in my experience, most spiritual folks have somewhere that they go to where they feel more connected to their chosen divinity.

For me, some of my favourite sacred spaces are simply spots within nature where I go to and stand or sit quietly. Sometimes I might take a small candle, light it, hold it, then take it away with me again. Other times, I will take some nuts as I know the squirrels and birds both appreciate them! I don't do this too regularly, as it's important for wild animals not to become reliant on humans feeding them.

One such spot is a crossroads of oak and silver birch trees at a hilly spot of ancient woodland, close to where I live. The energy I have felt rising up in that spot, with zero intervention from me, is quite breath-taking. The largest silver birch is old, and reaches out of the ground in a split trunk that resembles a great, cracked hand. The oaks range from saplings to elderly giants, and the acorns attract a variety of creatures to feast on their fallen remains. The whole place feels rich with life, and worthy of reverence.

Of course, not all sacred spaces are outdoors, and not all outdoor spaces are easily accessible. For those who stay indoors for ritual, meditation, or even moots and gatherings, there are lots of ways to do this in an environmentally conscious way.

Indoor Spaces

An indoor sacred space can be literally anywhere you choose. Whether you choose to create an altar or shrine, or designate a room for meditations or healings, or simply a space where you go to lose yourself in meditation or mindfulness, your sacred space is uniquely yours and you choose what happens there.

My indoor sacred space consists primarily of two altars. I have a triple layered altar for Hekate, near my front doorway, the most liminal and transitional place in the house. These three shelves represent earth, sea and sky, the realms She has dominion over. My altar decorations include carefully sourced statuary, shells, rocks, feathers, an old key, and cruelty-free candles. Pride of place is an antique set of scales that my husband picked up for me at a fair; they represent justice, one of her key virtues.

I also have an altar for the Mórrígan, close to the centre of my home. Items here include a decorated skull painted and given to me by my sibling, even more feathers (I like birds, can you tell?), a framed image given to me by a mentor, a pyrographed piece of wood with the image of a crow by a local artist, plus shells, foraged elderflowers in a re-purposed jar, and a pinecone. There is also a red candle in an old whiskey bottle, something we both enjoy.

Using old bottles and jars on a sacred altar is fine, just make sure you clean them thoroughly so that they don't attract bacteria or pests. You can even use different methods to sanctify items for your sacred space. Some people like to cleanse items in either moonlight or sunlight. Others may simply run them under water. Thoroughly cleaning and dabbing with an oil associated with your chosen divinity can be a way to create a clear connection between the now sacred object and your deity. I like to manually clean jars then sterilize them with steam or boiling water. They can then be sanctified (if necessary) and used for whatever purpose you like. As well as my elderflowers, I currently have jars around the house with dried crab-apples , rose petals, orchid petals and more – all gathered by me and all absolutely free. The orchid was a gift, and flowers every few years. I've had it for nearly two decades now, and only a small jar of flowers to show for it. I plan to use them as a catalyst in some magical working, perhaps something associated with passion and creativity.

You may be surprised at the number of things you already have to hand which you can use within your sacred space, saving you money but also being kind to the environment as you don't have to buy absolutely everything brand new, which use up resources, or have things delivered to your home, which increases greenhouse emissions.

Shared Sacred Space

When we get together, we like to be in venues which are comfortable and have plenty of great facilities. Moots, yoga classes, meditation groups; they all need suitable venues where people can relax and immerse themselves in the spirituality or community of the event. It may be tempting to grab the nearest or cheapest venue, but there are a few factors you might want to consider to ensure it's a good fit ethically as well as practically.

Accessibility

This point is about being kind to your fellow humans. I would hope that, as we move deeper into the 21st Century, most buildings would have good access for people with a range of abilities, from wheelchair users to those with limited sight. However, I know from sad experience that this is not the case, especially in older buildings where modifications have not been made. Give the venue a once over, ideally with someone who is disabled from your group, and check it's okay. Considerations may include:

- Ramps on every floor or easily accessible lifts
- Handrails
- A room where someone can go for a quiet moment in case of sensory overload
- Accessible toilets

- Braille or raised writing on any signs e.g. directions around the venue
- Consistent and clear signage
- Door handles, lift buttons, entry code pads etc. at a height accessible for wheelchair users
- Appropriate parking
- Induction loop systems where needed to help hearing aid users

There are probably many more considerations than this. The UK's National Disability Authority recommends buildings get an accessibility expert to audit the premises every three years. You could ask for the venue's most recent audit, and if they look at you blankly, it's probably not a good sign!

Don't just cater to the disabilities within your group right now. You may get different group members in the future, or one of your existing group could develop a disability or may even already have one that they haven't opened up to you about yet. Being inclusive helps everyone – a rising tide really does lift all boats.

Facilities

The main facilities that you need to consider when thinking about the environmental kindness of your venue are:

- Heat
- Water
- Waste

If your venue is always cold and you have to turn the heating up full at every session, that's a lot of power being used and a lot of emissions being produced somewhere.

Dripping taps or taps that run for ages after you turn them off, or that only run at a pace that's more like a hose pipe; these are very wasteful and also just downright annoying to deal with.

If you're prepared to take all your waste home with you, then this last point might not be too much of an issue. But it's probably worth checking that the building you're using has recycling facilities rather than just one single bin.

Of course, we can't all pick and choose the most amazing venues for our get-togethers. Sometimes choice is very limited, or funds might be an issue. You could always talk to the owner or landlord of the venue, and see if you can get them on board with making small changes. They might not, in their position, be aware of a drippy tap or a missing recycling bin, and may even appreciate your input.

Outdoor Spaces

At one of my most beloved spots where we gather as a tribe a few times a year, there is a wonderful sign always present at the entrance way. It says, in beautiful, stylised writing, "Leave Only Footprints". As a group, we take this very seriously, but also in our stride. Why would we want to leave our rubbish lying all over the gorgeous English countryside? Why would we wish to disrupt the local ecosystem, or cause harm to wildlife? I find this attitude prevalent among many local Pagan groups, and it fills me with hope for the future; that we don't find it a chore to be kind to our local and wider environment, we simply accept that it's the way things should be.

Sadly, what can happen at larger Pagan gatherings, is that the respect for our planet seems to wane against a sort of collective over-excitement. A poignant example of this is the littering that occurs one of the world's most famous sacred sites, Stonehenge, in Wiltshire, England. Every year, at the solstices, thousands of revellers come together at the famous standing stones to watch the sunrise. That sunlight sometimes illuminates a dreadful sight: a strew of cans, bottles, and plastic bags, and weary volunteers picking every piece up by hand. I cannot imagine visiting any UNESCO World Heritage Site, never mind one with such spiritual significance, and leaving so much as a fallen crisp packet.

I also get tears in my eyes when I see ribbons or cords tied around trees. Some folks might think it's a harmless and beautiful way to show honour to the local spirits or to make a wish. After all, wishing trees appear in folklore all over the world. Clootie wells in Ireland, Scotland, and the Isle of Man are sacred spots where supplicants wet a rag at the well, then tie the rag on a branch with a wish or a prayer. In Japan, during the Tanabata festival, people write their wishes on a piece of paper and hang it on a bamboo tree. In parts of Turkey, ribbons and nazar, a blue, glass amulet against the evil eye, are hung in trees for good luck. It's no wonder some people think it's a spiritual, wonderful thing to do. But the thing is, trees are growing, living organisms. As they grow, the ribbon or cord cuts into the branch or trunk, causing damage and putting the tree at risk of disease. Plus, many modern ribbons are synthetic, meaning they may never biodegrade or take hundreds of years to do so, producing toxic chemicals as they eventually break down. Just because something has been done for hundreds of years does not always mean it's a good idea. If you are enamoured with the idea of a wishing tree, why not make one with a branch which has already fallen from a tree? "Pot" it, so it stands like a tree. You could even add other branches and twigs, then decorate it however you like, or add a ribbon every time you want to make a prayer, petition, or wish.

Wherever you find your own outdoor sacred space, respect for the local environment has to be key. Sacred fires, large ritual gatherings, or just a simple nature walk can all have ramifications. They are all also fantastic ways to connect with the outside world and the elements, so it's about finding a balance that works for you. What are the most planet-friendly ways to enjoy an outdoor gathering?

- Ensure any fires are contained, safe, and absolutely away from plant life or wildlife habitats.
- If at all possible, have a fire marshal or experienced person to ensure the fire is extinguished at the appropriate time and that it never goes out of control.
- Never leave litter of any kind.
- If you have to leave offerings, ensure they are completely biodegradable and non-toxic.
- Bird seed, nuts, oats, or items you find at the site such as stones, leaves or feathers are completely acceptable and also wonderful as they show you are respecting the spirits of this place.
- This should go without saying, but never destroy or move anything you didn't create.
- That includes human-crafted structures like drystone walls or cairns, as they often become homes for wildlife.
- Think about how many folks you're bringing and the wear and tear on the local environment; three people in a grassy glade might make minimal impact, but 20 could tear up the turf and terrify the local wildlife, without even realising it.
- With that in mind, choose your location mindfully and with consideration to the local inhabitants.
- Pour libations onto bare earth only, as alcohol can damage plant life (more on that later).
- Never leave chocolate or other very sugary items as food offerings as they can be toxic to other animals.
- If you burn incense, do it in an open space and take any ashes or remnants home with you.
- Never tie anything around a living tree or shove anything into its roots.
- Likewise, don't wedge candles, gemstones, or other things you brought with you into drystone walls, holes in natural rock formations, cracks in the ground etc. You

might see it as a wonderful offering, but the chances are the spirits of that place will not be happy with you leaving what is basically litter. Carry with you no desire to leave your mark on this place; be open to the natural environment changing and influencing you, instead.

Because this is only scratching the surface of practicing paganism in an outdoor setting, I've explored the topic much more deeply later in the book in the chapter on *Outdoor Paganism*.

Action: If you have ever attended outdoor Pagan gatherings before, try and remember them and write down any ways in which you noticed the hosts or facilitators were being deliberately mindful and kind towards the environment. If you can, write these points down in a journal. Conversely, think of any times when you observed either a callousness or a thoughtlessness towards the local environs, even if it was via ignorance rather than malice. For each instance, think of why it happened, and how you could prevent it from happening if you attended or organised similar events in the future.

Ultimately, as the sign at our camp says, we aim to *leave only footprints*, as the enduring changes we want to experience after Pagan gatherings or ritual are in our hearts, minds, or spirits.

Eco-Friendly Offerings for your Sacred Space

Once of my favourite questions I was asked at a recent talk was what I would recommend for eco-friendly offerings. I found myself talking a great deal about researching what your deities or spirits want, where you will be providing these offerings, and how long those offerings will be hanging around for. There are many aspects of leaving offerings to the invisible beings in our lives, and your relationship with your divinities will be completely personal. I offer Hekate garlic, olive oil, and occasionally eggs. I know they are sacred to her, plus I can dispose of them in a way which is kind to the environment. If the garlic sprouts, it is planted. If it doesn't, I may leave it at the crossroads point in my garden. Eggs are fine to compost, but I highly recommend you remove them from the altar regularly, and don't bury them. Many, many years ago, I once buried an egg that had been on my Hekate alter. I subsequently forgot the exact place I had buried it, and whilst weeding weeks later, put the tines of the garden fork right through it. The foul smell that emerged from the ground was incredible! And we only had a tiny garden at the time, so it wafted straight into the house. Unpleasant is an understatement. Nowadays, I would thank the egg for its time on my sacred space, and crack it directly into the compost, then stir the compost.

Other ideas for easily disposable offerings include:

- Oats and oatcakes
- Seeds
- Grains
- Nuts
- Fruit
- Vegetables
- Shells
- Seaweed
- Driftwood
- Dried plants and flowers
- Herbs
- Stones
- Clean water and infused water, or water from a living source like a stream
- Keep alcohol to very small amounts

Head to the Resources section in the back of this book for more details on eco-friendly offering and discover which deities might appreciate what.

What to do with Used Offerings

There are a number of different ways to go here, and what you decide to do may depend on the type of offering and how long it has been in use.

Many offerings can be ritually buried. This is particularly appropriate for seeds and pinecones, and if a little tree grows, perhaps you can carefully rehome it or donate it to a local organisation. Small rocks and stones could also be buried, as long as you don't uproot or damage plants or the homes of small animals. Most food can also be buried as long as it's low in salt.

If you regularly have a fire anyway, you could burn anything that won't give off a toxic gas. This is particularly useful for spell work where words are written then burnt either to dispel their effect and extract them from your life, or to offer them up to a deity or spirit as some sort of commitment or worship.

You may also want to consider taking offerings such as nuts and seeds and moving them to a bird feeder – a most kind way to dispose of them. I don't know of any deity that would disapprove of this, but of course, follow your own path's guidance and your own instincts.

Libations can be poured away as long as they won't cause harm. We're usually only talking about very small amounts, but very strong alcohol can be harmful to both plants and wildlife. Consider watering down the libations before disposing of them or having a dedicated area in your yard or garden with excellent drainage, where nothing grows. For example, a rock garden with a gravel patch where you always pour them away.

Other food items may be left at sacred spot outdoors, if they are non-toxic. Avoid anything high in sugar or salt, and remember, chocolate can kill other animals, even though it tastes good to them. I sometimes use a small piece of oatcake as an offering, which I then leave at a special spot in my garden. Whether it's the birds or the local spirits that take it, who knows?

Action: Do you leave any sort of offerings in your practice?

Think about them or make a list. Can you dispose of them effectively and kindly when needed? If not, what alternatives are there, that still honour your deities or spirits in the best way? There might not be an alternative – and that's okay. We make changes where we can, and don't feel guilty when there is no option for change.

Chapter 5

Self Sufficiency for Spiritual Growth

Chop it, cut it, scrape it, grate it
Soak it in vinegar
Don't waste it
Too much has already
Been chucked in the bin
We keep starting again
And
again
And again
But some of these fruits and vegetables

Are still good
A little soft
A little wobbly
A little less sweet
Just add some sugar
And soak it in
vinegar
Let the sharp bubbles
Oxymoronically float
To the surface
While all the good stuff
Is preserved
Colour and flavour and aroma
All infusing the juice
And the room
Like I pickled the house
Like I soaked it in vinegar
These beets and roots

These leaves and fruits
Past their best but still
Worth something
Soak them in vinegar
Give them as gifts
For not everything has to be perfect
In order to bring joy.

As I mentioned in the first chapter, we are nowhere near wholly self-sufficient as a household. I don't imagine that many folks in modern, Western society are. What I aim for, in my daily life and my own personal learning, is to develop new ways that allow me to move a little closer to self-sufficiency. We joke, within our tribe, that we all have something to offer when the zombie apocalypse comes. Some of us can fix things. One knows how to mill wood in straight planks. Another can sew, knot, and crochet better than anyone else I know. Another is the most amazing baker. Still more folks have various first aid and healing skills that always end up coming in useful when we are away at camps and trips out. Plus, there's a variety of entertainment skills within our group, from guitar to storytelling, so we're never bored.

My own skills bring me an enormous sense of wellbeing, a sense of pride in myself and my skills that moves beyond ego and into what I can offer to my community. Should we ever end up in a position where we had to fend for ourselves, I know that I have a fair knowledge of the following skills:

- Preserving
- Pickling
- Cooking
- Herbal medicine
- Massage both for physical therapy and relaxation
- Aromatherapy
- Music

- Poetry
- Composting
- Botany, in particular knowledge of herbs, fruits and vegetables
- Various forms of witchcraft and magic

Even if only one of these skills ever comes in handy in that hypothetical apocalypse, I'll be proud of myself for having learnt it. It will probably be the preserving skill, because everyone loves the jam! With every skill I learn and practice, my belief in myself and my confidence increases. No matter what path you walk, you cannot deny the power of those feelings of self-worth. They can carry you through difficult times and allow you to stand strong in the face of adversity.

Of course, the added bonus of learning to make things yourself or fix things yourself is that you usually end up being kinder to the environment. When my husband fixes our taps himself, we don't have to hire a plumber, which means less traffic on the roads and fewer car fumes. When I make my own jam out of fruit from the local food waste initiative, I'm preventing food from going into landfill or compost, and by not buying it at the supermarket, less jars have to be made, and that's protecting our natural resources.

Sometimes the impact we make with these small changes in our lives isn't immediately obvious. When you stop and think about anything you do by hand, you'll probably find that it has a positive knock-on effect somewhere along the line.

Learning a Skill

I was astonished when I was researching this book, to discover the array of skills that abound in the Pagan community. I've seen handmade altar cloths made from unwanted clothes, carefully embroidered until they are indistinguishable from many of the "professionally" made items at major stores. In fact, they're better, as they're completely personal to the crafter and their particular path. I've seen gorgeous bowls made entirely from glue and autumn leaves. This was like real magic. The crafter in question had formed the leaves around an existing bowl, layered them with glue, and allowed it to dry thoroughly before gently removing the original bowl. The resulting item was like leaves levitating into a bowl shape of their own accord, and by all accounts, surprisingly strong!

As well as crafting and making things with your hands, there are any number of skills which you can learn and apply on your sacred path. I love to write poems, and use poetry a great deal within my practice. I'm currently working on a book of verse dedicated to the Tuatha Dé Danann, deities or very powerful beings of ancient Ireland. This has been an ongoing project for some time, and I'm not sure it will be finished any time soon; as with many sacred undertakings, it's as much about the journey as the finished project. One of my favourite pieces calls on imagery of crows, sacred to the Mórrígan and her sisters, and snippets from some of the most famous stories of the Tuatha Dé Danann.

There's a black feather floating on the wind
Gasp it in, sigh it out
Breath of blood, hot iron in my nostrils
Suck it in, steam it out
Long red hair that catches on the fence post
Tie it back, pull it out
Great club beating on the fractured bed rock
Call him o'er, call him out
Passion spanning over secret rivers
Hold it in, let it out
Pacts and wars are sealed with silver kisses
Throw it in, hurl it out
Death of hero, dog meat bile in belly,
Gulp it in, spew it out

Crows are circling; Badb, Macha and Nemain;
Hear them out
Hear them out
Hear them out.

When I've finished the book, it will be an offering in its own right. I do the same with music. I write devotional songs, sometimes in response to something that has happened or is going to happen. I prayed to Hekate Einalian, the oceanic aspect of this Goddess, to protect us on a journey across the sea once. I was glad I did, as it was very stormy and quite alarming. In return, I wrote a song about my experience and my devotion, and sang it live at my next gig. I have also created chants, for clearing the mind before ritual or meditation, and any number of songs celebrating the natural world and the turn of the season. I play most of these on the acoustic guitar, so other than the materials used in making the guitar, singing and writing is a completely eco-friendly way to honour my deities. You don't need to have the voice of an angel to make music – I certainly don't! You could try:

- Banging a drum
- Making a rattle from an old crisp tube or coffee tin, with some dried beans or rice in
- Humming or whistling
- Clapping
- Dancing or spinning, moving your body in joyful ways
- Chanting
- Wailing or shouting to raise energy

Action: What are your skills? Educational establishments and some workplaces now often get students or employees to write a comprehensive list of their skills. This allows them to see what skills are transferable between jobs or areas of study, and to feel a sense of achievement when a new skill is added to that list.

Include any skills you like. They don't have to all be related to your spirituality. Ask someone you know really well to look over it for you; I bet at least one person will tell you of a skill you've forgotten to add! Reflect on how much you're already capable of, and create a goal of learning something you've always wanted to know how to do. I'm currently learning Spanish with my son, and figuring out the intricacies of sourdough.

Making Your Own

Hobbies like crafting and cooking become extra practical when you're able to make things that you use in your day to day life. These might be edible items, like my ever-present jam, or alternatives to store-bought items. A good example is waxing cloth and using it as reusable coverings for food instead of clingfilm. This reduces plastic use and, if you ever do need to throw one away, fabrics like cotton biodegrade much faster than plastic-based cling film or Saran Wrap. You can also make your own items for use within your spiritual practice.

Candles

Candles are something that are fun to make and useful for meditation, ritual, or simply providing soft light to any room where you need to rest and reflect. You can even collect the ends of candles which won't burn any further, and melt them down, combining the used wax to make more new candles.

There are a number of ways to make candles, from rolling a sheet of beeswax around a wick, to dipping wicks over and over in melted wax until a candle forms around the wick. If you're vegan, beeswax might not be an option so you may want to consider soy wax or coconut wax. Just be mindful about where the wax comes from, and how it's grown. Soy production can use tons of pesticides and contribute to deforestation and the destruction of natural habitats (WWF, 2016) so look out for certifications like RTRS, the Roundtable on Responsible Soy.

Palm oil is another additive in candles that can be problematic, so again, check that your wax supplier uses sustainable sources.

Poppets

Small doll or human figurines have been used in magic and seasonal celebrations all over the world for many centuries. If you're interested in poppet magic, I highly recommend Lucya Starza's book, *Pagan Portals: Poppets and Magical Dolls*. You can create a poppet with bits of old fabric, very basic sewing skills, and anything you like to stuff them with. This might include more pieces of fabric, herbs, or even small tokens like rocks or feathers associated with the magic you're trying to create. You could even use modelling clay, or pieces of grass to create an approximately human shape. If you're especially artistic, you could try and create a sculpture of a deity or spirit that you have a relationship. I once went to a wood whittling class at a Pagan festival, and tried to "release the spirit" within the small, foraged branch I was provided with. Either the spirit was quite happy where it was, or I simply have zero flare for whittling; I lean towards the latter! I still have the piece, though, to remind me of the fun I had trying something new.

Symbols

Many spiritual paths employ a range of symbols. I'm currently learning more about the Ogham, an ancient Irish writing system. Tragically, we recently had to have a silver birch tree cut down in our back garden as it was causing damage to a neighbour's home. I kept the wood, unwilling to simply let it be burned or mulched. I plan to use some of that wood to make my own set of Ogham letters. The alphabet in Ogham starts with *Beith*, which means birch, so I think this is going to be a really appropriate use of the wood. I'll use pyrography to burn the symbols into the wood, and hope that having a set of the letters I can use again and again will help me to learn them and their meanings more effectively.

Other symbols and sets of symbols commonly employed in paganism include Norse runes, elemental symbols for earth, air, fire, and water, ancient Egyptian symbols such as an Ankh or the Eye of Horus, labyrinths, or symbols representing specific aspects of nature such as trees, birds, rocks, mountains, or particular deities or spirits. Of course, that's not an exhaustive list, and your own path may use a whole slew of symbols that I've not touched upon here. Whatever those symbols happen to be, I can almost guarantee that there will be some expensive and resource-heavy items based on them in just about any major online retailer. Making your own is so much more personal, and much, much kinder to the environment. You don't have to be an expert with pyrography tools either. Options include:

- Drawing the symbols on paper or card
- Painting them
- Marking them on rocks
- Making them out of other items in fixed or moveable collages or mosaics
- Carving them into wood or other materials
- Making them out of modelling materials like clay

There's something very mindful about concentrating on the task of making the symbols that mean something to you. Knowing that you help the planet by doing so adds even more meaningful energy to that accomplishment.

Growing Your Own

What would any chapter on self-sufficiency be without a section on growing your own produce? I absolutely adore growing things, so find it endlessly frustrating that I'm not actually the best at it! I've got a terrible memory and forget to do important gardening tasks like weeding and watering. I get bogged down in other tasks, then when it comes to sorting out the garden, suddenly there are a hundred little jobs to do that make it seem insurmountable. Like anything, looking after a garden, allotment, or other green space is easier when you do a little every day. This is something I'm still working on.

Not everyone has access to a garden or patch of ground to grow things in, but if you have even one windowsill that gets a bit of light, you can grow herbs or have a houseplant. Plants improve our indoor air quality, and are awesome for our mental health. Studies show that interacting with indoor plants can reduce both physiological and psychological stress (Lee, Lee, Park, and Miyazaki, 2015). I have cacti on the windowsill in the kitchen. They take such little looking after, yet they make me happy.

If you do have the space, the easiest and most practical plants to grow indoors are, probably, herbs. Depending on where in the world you are, you might have access to different seeds. Indoors, I grow coriander and parsley, as the weather is too unpredictable to depend on putting them in the garden. Seeds in moist compost should germinate easily. Don't overwater them, and don't let them completely dry out. A middle ground is best for most herbs.

Outdoors I have rosemary, marjoram, lovage, mint, and an amazing smelling plant called the dwarf curry plant. I had lavender, but they were baby plants and fell victim to cats digging! I use many of these herbs in my practice, either as offerings or in magic work. Towards the end of this book, I've listed a few correspondences for common herbs. I use rosemary for memory boosting, as well as cleansing and protection. I use mint to refresh the mind and for clarity. If you have fresh herbs, it means you can take what you need as and when you need it. Don't take so much that that the plant can't recover. Most herbs are "cut and come again" meaning they won't miss a few leaves here or there. For seasonal herbs, you can cut and dry some before the season runs out. Another storage option is to chop herbs and freeze them. For culinary purposes, mixing chopped herbs into oil then freezing them in ice cube trays is a great way to have your favourite herbs all winter long.

Flowers are another thing you can grow yourself rather than buying. Although I never complain when my husband returns home with a bunch of flowers when he's been shopping! Many flowers are associated with deities or particular traditions and folklore. I have columbines at the top of my garden, and as the weather warms, I'm treated to beautiful red and cream flowers that almost dance in the breeze. The flowers are associated with clarity and courage, and the Latin name *Aquilegia* comes from the word for Eagle. I don't pick the flowers are they are simply too gorgeous in situ, but as they start to fade, I try and gather the petals as they fall. I might put them around me as I meditate for greater clarity on a particular situation.

Some vegetable and fruits can be grown indoors too, like chilli peppers or tomatoes. I reckon I could probably live off chillies and tomatoes, at a push. I love spicy food; I can't get enough of it! One of my favourite things to make for seasonal gifts is chilli jam, which is basically just bell peppers, chilli peppers, vinegar and sugar. It looks like stained glass and tastes amazing. As well as the culinary uses, there are the associations like love, passion, creativity and the element of fire which make chilli a useful part of many magical practices.

Outdoors you can grow a variety of vegetables depending on the climate where you live. Sometimes it doesn't even matter what you grow. The simple act of feeling the soil under you or in your fingers, or watching something grow from practically nothing into a full grown plant; it's so satisfying and I personally feel it's one of the finest ways to connect to the Earth and understand the turning of the seasons.

Foraging

Garlic mustard, Jack by the Hedge
Found in verges, wasteland, the edge
Of towns and streets, yet growing wild
A plant which is anything but mild
The leaves are pungent, tasty too
And used in salad, sauce, and stew.
With pointy leaves and flowers white,
Jack keeps our verges looking bright.

If you're able to get out and about in your local area, you may be very surprised to find that there are plenty of "free food" options available. Now, I need to start by saying *never* eat anything you are not absolutely 100% about. If you have any doubt at all, simply don't do it. It's not worth getting sick over. I would also add that unless you are an absolute expert, avoid mushrooms and fungi. So many varieties are very similar in appearance, yet one might be perfectly edible and tasty whilst another might kill you.

You can look out for foraging courses, either online or in your local area, or you can join various groups via social media. I'm a member of a foraging group and a group that specialises in identifying wild plants all over the world; two groups that work very well together. The aforementioned Jack by the Hedge is prolific in my area, and extremely useful as a source of nutrients and flavour. It makes lovely pesto. Other useful plants in my area are dandelions, rowan berries, hawthorn berries, rosehips, elderflowers and elderberries, cherries, plums, apples, and salsify. What grows around your home?

Incense

Incense burning for ritual or religious purposes is a practice that is thousands of years old and spans a variety of cultures. Incense comes in a variety of forms including sticks, loose incense to burn on charcoal, or little cones. Flameless fragrance is an option for those that can't have smoke in the house, for example, due to asthma.

You can make incense with the simplest of ingredients. You don't have to spend a fortune on expensive resins and powders if you don't want to. If you can grow any of the ingredients yourself, even better! Ingredients that you can burn in homemade loose incense include:

- Rosemary
- Rose flowers
- Lavender
- Asafoetida (small amounts)
- Cinnamon (small amounts, perhaps better for outdoor burning as cinnamon smoke can irritate some people)
- Pine resin – you can often find it on the trunks of pine trees and peel it off like glue
- Sage (culinary or home-grown; I don't advocate sourcing exotic strains of sage as they're not always sustainable or culturally appropriate)
- Allspice
- Juniper berries
- Citrus fruit peel like lime, lemon or orange
- Dried apple
- Chamomile
- Various tree bark – we often find strips of bark on the ground where squirrels have been feeding

Bread

Bread of all kinds can be made in the home, from crusty, white loaves to specialty breads flavoured with fruits, nuts, seeds, honey and more. Bread is a popular choice as an offering within various spiritual practices precisely because it can be modified and personalised so much. Making bread by hand is a very mindful activity. The kneading and shaping can become soothing and repetitive, allowing your deeper mind to work through problems and find answers. If you can't knead bread by hand, bread made in a maker is just as good and you can still personalise it as much as you like.

Stars or Pentagrams

It's very simple to make a basic wooden star out of fallen wigs and string. Simply find five twigs of a similar diameter and length, or cut or break them to the same length. Arrange them into the classic five pointed star shape, with each end of the twig slightly crossing over the next. At the junctions where the twig cross, firmly wrap twine or string, ensuring the twigs stay at the correct angle to form the star. Once complete, you can decorate further with berries, leaves, paper ornaments, or anything you like. These make fantastic winter solstice decorations, or a simple way to make a pentagram for your altar or sacred space. Once you get the hang of making shapes with twigs, you're not limited to stars. Use your imagination and creativity to make something that's specific to you and your path.

Finding ways to create, grow, and entertain are core aspects of humanity, so it's no wonder that we attach such spiritual significance to them. Music and poetry; food and the ability to provide for each other; the joy of making something beautiful from basic components; all these things come together to create a cross cultural language that breaks down barriers wherever it is nurtured.

Chapter 6

Switching Up: Small Change for Big Impact

There's no getting away from the fact that we all have to be more mindful about how we live our lives. The planet is changing, and the climate is becoming more unpredictable and volatile with every passing year. Being a Pagan of any path means having a connection to the world at some level, and I've certainly deeply felt the changes in recent years. Living in the UK, a seasonal and temperate country, autumn and spring in particular are different to how they used to be. The weather around the equinoxes is wetter, warmer and stormier.

Whether or not you believe these changes are temporary or part of a wider climate change crisis, there is nothing to be lost by being kinder to the planet. Of course, this applies to everyone - not just Pagans. But to reiterate my key point, I hope, as Pagans, that we have a common sense of responsibility towards the world.

In my first coven, we used to end every ritual with the pledge that we would only take as much from this world as we could reasonably hope to give back. In other words, we won't take more from Planet Earth than it can manage. We won't deplete the Earth's resources deliberately, and if we have to take, we'll find ways to help the Earth replenish herself. This might be by switching a product you use, finding a better or different way to do something, or actively working to give back.

Switching Up: Pagan Tools and Accessories

If you examine the paraphernalia of your spiritual path and discover that some of it comes from far away or isn't sourced as ethically as you'd like, please don't immediately start throwing things away! Those things then become waste, adding to the problems of landfill or energy usage, plus the object in question can no longer be of use. If you look at something and think, "There's no way I would buy that now!", great! We can only do better when we know better. However, if you still get use out of the item, that's wonderful and you should continue to do so. In fact, the longer the item's life, the more positive its influence becomes, as it helps you reduce your consumption. If you do decide to get rid of things, skip back to Chapter 2 for more information on letting go of things with gratitude.

Some of the most commonly purchased Pagan or esoteric items, according to various online stores and outlets, include:

- Jewellery
- Art and sculpture including deities, other supernatural beings, and skulls
- Decorative trinkets such as jars filled with sand and shells or wreaths
- Candles
- Incense burners
- Cauldrons
- Wax seals
- Incense
- Tarot cards
- Runes
- Spell kits
- Moon phase calendars and clocks
- Stickers and decals (think things like, "My Other Car is a Broom")
- Crystals
- Decorative boxes and bowls
- Pendulums

Now you might read through that list and thing, "why would I buy *that*?", which is my reaction to many of those things.

However, I have absolutely bought some of them in the past. I buy tarot cards, because I don't have the skill or talent to make my own. I have been given spell kits to use and review, although I've never bought them myself. I have bought incense sticks for convenience, although I do tend to make my own loose incense nowadays. I might buy a laptop sticker, but it won't be from a major outlet. I've found some Irish Paganism specific ones from eelandotter.com which I am in love with, and I know the money goes towards a small business with good ethics, which makes me happy.

There are alternatives to buying many of these items from the "big" shops. Depending on what you use in your path, the following alternatives might help you make more environmentally kind choices along the way

Tools

This broad title covers everything from athames to wands, to bells and candles, to scrying balls and pendulums. There is a huge and growing trend on social media platforms like Instagram to share glamourous shots of altars, in a kind of one-upmanship of "look at all the shiny things I have!". Just go and browse through the hashtag *#WitchesOfInstagram* and you'll see what I mean. Don't get me wrong, there's some awesome posts in there too. But the aesthetic and the need to draw followers seems to run ahead of the potential consequences of the consumerist nature of some of these posts. For me, a gorgeous autumn day with trees or running water is much more glamourous.

Needless to say, while I appreciate that anyone can share whatever they want online, I don't think ensuring you have the latest, shiniest accessories on your altar is very planet-friendly and I would *love* to see a new trend emerge. How about *#upcycledaltar* or *#thriftwitchery*? One can dream!

There are so many tools used by so many Pagans, and so many Pagans who don't see the need for tools of any kind. There is, of course, no right or wrong with this. The beauty of Paganism is its diversity, so if this section doesn't apply to you, feel free to move on.

I have a friend, a powerful witch, who once raised her eyebrow then her finger, saying, "This is my wand." For her, that was so true. For others, a tool is a point of focus for the will or energy, or it might be symbolic, linked to a particular tradition or deity, or simply for purely practical purposes. I've tried to list a few tools I've come across in my own practice as a Celtic-inspired witch and Hellenic practitioner, plus tools I know are popular amongst other Pagan paths. If you don't see your own favourite tools here, take a moment to think about them and if they have an eco-friendly alternative. If not, and they are tools you need, that's okay. You can find ecological balance in other ways.

Athame or Boline

These are two types of ritual knives used in Wicca and some eclectic practices. I've never had one, not being a Wiccan, but I've seen plenty over the years and even been trusted to handle one a couple of times. A common practice among friends was to source the blade from a smith, and craft the handle themselves. Alternatively, on some occasions the person wanting the athame would find the piece of wood that felt right to them, and give it to a craftsperson to turn it into the handle of a knife. I've also seen handles made carefully out of modelling clay, the kind that can be fired to a hard, glossy finish. Sometimes these handles are hand painted or carved with runes or other symbols.

Pendulum

I've never bought a pendulum in my life. The first pendulum I ever made was with a plait of my own hair and a teardrop shaped stone from a favourite necklace. And it worked! Look out for independent sellers who can tell you where the materials for the pendulum come from and how they are sourced.

Altar Cloths

There are so many fabulous altar cloths out there. Altar cloths are generally one piece of fabric designed to cover an altar, shrine, or other sacred space, and can be black, brightly coloured, embroidered, or very simple. All my altar cloths are either gifts or charity shop/thrift store finds. My favourite is a sarong a friend gave me, which is deep blue with tiny mirrors embroidered into it. I love the way the light catches on it from the nearby window; it feels joyful and draws the eye, reminding me gently of my commitments. I also have a dark red scarf which cost me a couple of pounds (sterling) from a charity shop. Someone took the effort to donate it instead of letting it go to landfill, I bought it, knowing that money I spent would go to a good cause, and now it gets used 6 out of 12 months as I alternate it with my other favourites. You can buy altar cloths from local craftspeople, online from independent sellers, or make your own from disused or waste fabric.

Yoga Mats

Lots of people love yoga mats or similar, even if they don't practice themselves. They can provide a comfortable place to sit or lay whilst meditating, or whilst kneeling or sitting to worship, or just to take some time out to reflect and rest. Sadly, many yoga mats are made of PVC, a plastic which uses non-renewable resources and doesn't really biodegrade once it has to be thrown away. It's not all bad news: one PVC yoga mat should last many years if treated well, so it reduced the need to replace and buy more. But there are alternatives. Look out for yoga mats made of natural, sustainable materials. Some brands promise to plant a tree for every mat they sell, offsetting any emissions made during the production of the mats. Most companies are very transparent about the sustainable efforts they are making – after all it's great for their brand reputation – so be sure to do a bit of research before making a commitment.

Cauldrons

A cauldron is basically a large pot, usually made of cast iron or another metal. There's not a great deal you can do in terms of the materials if you're buying one, but you can save some emissions by buying locally either in store or from an online store that doesn't have to ship it very far. You can also use any suitable pot you have already as a substitute cauldron. The main question to consider is what you want to use your cauldron for. I have had three cauldrons in my time. The first was a silver bowl with "jewels" (chunks of glass) around the outside that I was drawn to like a magpie in my early twenties. I burnt incense in it and eventually ruined it as it wasn't really suitable for the task at hand. I then bought a maslin pan, which is a large and very robust pan designed for making jam and other preserves. I burnt this one irreparably while actually making jam in it. Years later, I finally have a tiny, cast iron cauldron with a lid and legs, ideal for burning incense in, and bought from a local esoteric shop. I use it to represent the Dagda on my altar, and the most it ever holds now is some feathers. Isn't it strange how our practice changes over time? If a cauldron sits well with your path, find one that suits your purposes now, and perhaps any future purpose you think you might use one for.

Bells

Bells can be used in ritual, to signify transitional points within meditation or pathworking, or to announce the presence of yourself or another being. They are also associated with exorcism. I have one bell. I've had it since I was a child. It's made of brass, it has a ship's wheel above the bell (years before I would begin my worship of Hekate Einalian, her oceanic aspect), and it originally came from a charity shop so is probably at least 45 years old if not much older. Definitely check out your local charity shop or thrift store if you want a bell. You might be able to find an old school bell, or even an antique ship's bell. If you buy a brand new bell, see if you can support your local music store or educational supplier, rather than buying from one of the major online retailers.

Herbs

We've already talked about growing your own, but there may be times when you need something a little more exotic or it may not be possible for you to grow your own. Good things to look out for are if the herbs are being grown organically, as pesticides or herbicides in your herbs may taint whatever use you have planned for them. Also consider where they are grown, how far they have to be shipped, and how sustainable they are; for example, ginseng is now classed as vulnerable and is protected in North America. Finally, avoid culturally significant herbs and plants such as white sage or Palo Santo unless you have the right to use them.

Books

E-books are a wonderful thing. Oh, I know how wonderful the smell of a *real* paper book is, and the satisfactory rustle of a page turn. I have hundreds of books in my house, but most of them predate the advent of the e-reader. I still buy a select few. If I spot a book at a second-hand store that I've wanted for ages, I will snap it up. I also adore recipe books and books about space or nature with glorious, colourful pictures. But mostly, I feel happy to have one device that holds more books than my house could ever hope to store. Plus, with the number of books I buy, I feel as if there are trees somewhere sighing in relief at my decision to turn to e-books as a modern solution. Using the e-reader app on your phone is even more eco-friendly, as a separate e-reader has a carbon footprint of around 168kg in its lifetime (Hutsko, 2009). Be sure to only download e-books from legitimate websites, as supposedly "free" e-books that shouldn't be often contain viruses or malware. Plus, it's nice for us authors to get paid!

The Crystal Controversy

Crystals are beautiful, incredible pieces of our planet with a multitude of uses. Many folks use them for healing, psychological boosts, and energetic work. They're even used to help practitioners feel more connected to the Earth from whence they came. Sadly, the Earth may be suffering because of the dramatically rising interest in crystals and crystal healing, which has come about in part thanks to celebrities touting their potential uses as aids for everything from singing to vaginal health.

Crystals are a non-renewable resource, many of them having been formed during the Earth's creation. More and more intensive mining to find new sources means worse conditions for labourers, who are already overworked and underpaid, and working in highly unsafe conditions. Mining, as we've touched on earlier in the book, has an enormous ecological impact. Plus, the industry is completely unregulated. Suppliers don't have to tell you where crystals came from or how they were sourced – and often don't (Wiseman, 2019). Some individual sellers will go out of their way to ensure their crystals are more ethically sourced. However, the simple truth is that the original supplier never has to disclose this information, making ethical crystal selling enormously difficult to implement or maintain.

As with everything, the better you know, the better you do. If you buy crystals, check with your supplier that they are ethically sourced. If they can't provide you with this information, try hunting around for a supplier that can. You could consider buying second-hand crystals and cleansing them to use for your own purposes. You could find used pieces of jewellery housing gemstone or crystals, and remove the stones from their settings. Or you could find alternatives, such as beautiful rocks from the beach, or if you're lucky enough, gemstones and minerals that you find yourself. On the beaches of England, I've found jet, quartz, and marble, and I bet there were many others I failed to identify at the time.

Switching up to eco-friendly versions of the things you do already can be as simple as finding a seller who is a little bit closer, or the same item but in a more sustainable material. Or it could be about making a major change in your life to make your entire practice more environmentally kind.

Action: What tools do you use in your regular practice? Do you have everything you need? When is the next time you might have to replace something? If you think you have everything you need and it will all last for many years, that's great, and it's a big achievement. If you have consumables within your practice, or items that need replacing, what can you do to make that process more eco-friendly? Even one small change here can have a big impact.

Chapter 7:

Outdoor Paganism

Paganism is a living faith, a collection of generally nature-based religions followed by people from all walks of life. One major delight I have found most Pagans have in common is a love of the outdoors. Depending on physical ability, many Pagans adore heading into the countryside, or to campsites, sacred spaces, stone circles, outdoor moots, meetings, and gatherings in settings where nature can be truly be appreciated.

Even city-dwelling Pagans often gather in parks or larger gardens, simply to breathe under the sky with their feet on the Earth. During 2020, in the times of social distancing, outdoor gatherings became even more important as for some it was the only way to meet up with likeminded people – at least at times when restriction allowed. I'm actually writing this section during the second week of the second lockdown in England, where we are only allowed to go outdoors in our own household "bubbles". I saw an amazing thing today, though. On the Royal Society for the Protection of Birds (RSPB) website, their tagline is "Nature is Still Open." Yes, yes it is.

Nature seems to be calling folks back to it in droves, so it's more important than ever that we learn how to be respectful towards it. There are some general guidelines about how to behave in the countryside, in fact, in the UK we have something called the countryside code published by Natural England. Much of this is about being courteous and thoughtful towards those who live in the countryside; don't block gates, keep out of the way of farm animals, slow down for horses and so forth. But there are some guidelines in there that affect the other inhabitants of our countryside; the ones who were there first.

Stick to the Paths

I can't hear this phrase without immediately returning to the movie *An American Werewolf in London*. Brusque locals warn a pair of hapless backpackers, "Stay on the road; keep clear of the moors." Of course, they follow neither of these pieces of advice and, well, I won't spoil the film for you should you not have seen it, but things take a bad turn from that point onward! Thankfully, in most easily accessible countryside areas, paths tend to be clearly marked; no ominous warnings required. And there are various reasons why sticking to these paths is good for both you and the nature you're travelling through.

If everyone sticks to the same paths, those paths become more well-worn which normally makes them easier to pick out. As well as being more recognisable, they are more likely to be tended to by local authorities to keep them in good condition and accessible. A council is unlikely to put a handrail or smooth surface on a tiny, winding trail, but they might consider it for a wide, well-worn path to help give people of various abilities and backgrounds access to beautiful green spaces.

Another benefit of sticking to paths is that it designates clearly which parts of the countryside humans have access to. It's worth remembering that we don't automatically have a *right* to wander the woods, the mountains, the plains, the deserts, or the seashore, especially not disrespectfully. Other things live there, and were there first in many cases. Sticking to a few paths rather than making multiple trails all over these natural habitats helps nature thrive in its natural environment.

Action: If you get the chance to go outdoors, next time you're on a path, stop, and examine both edges of the path. Can you see where human interaction ends? What's the first sign of plant life? Can you see any animal life? Appreciating the minutia of your journey into nature helps you understand just what a massive impact simply moving off a path could have. You might see delicate wildflowers, ants, or a sac of spider eggs. Take some photos or draw some pictures, or make a journal entry, as a way to stay connected to this moment.

Keep Dogs or Other Pets Under Control

There will, hopefully, be places which are suitable for dog owners to let them off the leash and run, play, and generally get some exercise and have some fun. It's important to be mindful that dogs dashing off through woodlands or on mountain paths, unsupervised, can cause damage or get hurt themselves. Small animals and nesting birds are particularly at risk.

Many coastal areas will have guidelines about when you can and can't take your dog on particular parts of the beach or shoreline. This is normally in line with nesting seasons, but there may be areas where cliffs or paths are not safe, too. Be aware of local signage and report inadequate or unclear signage, to support the rest of your community.

Fire Safety

Pagans practicing outdoors might often want a fire, either for warmth or for sacred purposes. In the countryside, a fire can have devastating consequences, as evidenced by the shocking Californian wildfire started in September 2019. This fire was at a popular camping area, and all it took was a badly designed firework to start a spark which destroyed over 7,000 acres of forest. That's a tragic amount of damage. If you have to have a fire in the woods, be sure it's permitted; make sure you're in line with local rules and guidelines; if unsure check with local authorities; and as stated earlier in the book, if you don't know what you're doing with fire, please don't just have a go and hope for the best. It really isn't worth the potential destruction that can come from a badly built or tended fire.

There are, of course, safe ways to have a fire outdoors, the primary one being to have an expert on hand who understands the technicalities and risks of fire building. Consider using a dedicated fire pit to avoid the fire being able to spread. If you start a fire directly on the ground, ensure it is just bare earth for several feet around the fire.

Ensure you are not starting the fire under overhanging branches or other flammable material. Have something on hand to smother the fire with should it start to get out of control. If alcohol or other substances are likely to make an appearance at your event, make sure the person in charge of the fire commits to staying sober.

Don't spray flammable liquids on the fire. Go through fire safety tips with everyone present. Make sure folks know what can and can't go on the fire. This is especially important for sacred fires for which it may be disrespectful to burn certain substances, but also protects the environment by avoiding toxic fumes if people try to burn plastic wrappers.

A fire can be a wonderful, communal centre to any group gathering. You can tell stories around it, toast marshmallows, and enjoy the outdoors at night. That's why it's such a good idea to ensure that someone within your group knows how to build and look after one properly.

Be Mindful of the Season

The countryside can change dramatically throughout the season, depending upon where you are in the world. In the UK, spring and autumn are both wet and windy, while summer can be either a deluge or a drought – or most commonly, both! In winter, temperatures drop but snow is sporadic; some years see massive, long lasting snow storms and cold spells like 2018's "Beast from the East." I find it fascinating when travelling to other places like the Canary Islands, for example, that their seasons are completely different. The changes are much more subtle, and there are microclimates dotted all over the islands where the weather barely ever changes. I appreciate, therefore, that everyone's experience of the turn of the seasons is different.

Wherever you live and whatever the climate is like, it's worth finding out how seasonal change affects the local flora and fauna in your favourite outdoor haunts. During springtime, we love to go down to some local woods to see the bluebells. But we wouldn't recommend going there with dogs off the leash, as they can trample on the delicate flowers and damage them.

Likewise, areas that have birds nesting may be off limits if you're planning a big, noisy ritual or gathering. March to July can be a busy time for birds of many species, so bear that in mind when you plan your outdoor gatherings. You might want to find out if there are any ground nesting birds in the areas you practice, as these are particularly vulnerable to hikers, dog walkers, and nature lovers of all kinds. One of my favourite birds is the curlew, instantly recognisable by its long, curved beak and the whooping calls it makes that give the bird its name. The curlew is currently a bird of global conservation concern, partly to do with dwindling nesting sites. Curlews nest on grassland and in meadows, so can easily be disrupted by foot traffic of any kind. Their nests are often partially hidden in tall grasses, making it easy for them to get trampled by curious explorers. Yet another great reason to stick to the paths unless you have intimate knowledge of the area and its inhabitants.

It is tempting, as Pagans or outdoor spiritual practitioners, to look for the most remote and off-the-grid place possible to practice, away from prying eyes and judgmental passers-by. However, it's almost guaranteed that some other living being has got there first, so please respect that this is their space, and not yours.

Action: If you are able to get outside and connect with your faith, write a short plan of how you would do it in an environmentally friendly way. Think about what this means in terms of the environment you are moving into. Do you need to take transport? Will you be solo or with others? Can you car share? Is it close enough to travel without a car, if you're able to do this? Once there, what will you need to disturb? Can you reasonably put things back after? Could your worship or sacred practice happen without any impact on the local environment at all, and if not as is sometimes the case), what could you do to offset any impact you have?

For example, you may worry that you are disturbing birds during the nesting season if you perform an outdoor ritual in the woods in spring. As well as keeping your work as quiet and unobtrusive as possible, you could offset this by making a donation or offering your time to an appropriate charity such as the RSPB (UK), Woodland Trust (UK), or American Bird Conservancy. Raising awareness or even making notes on how to adjust your spiritual practice is also a way to connect and commit to doing better, if you feel you need to do so.

For many Pagans, getting outside and feeling really connected to nature is a major part of their practice. Being able to do this whilst being kind to the other beings that live in these stunning and still strangely mysterious environments can surely only deepen that connection.

Chapter 8

Building a Community

Circle we dreamed
Seen in a haze
"One of these days..."
We banished that phrase

Circle we saw
In places we'd been
That made us feel keen
To make what we'd seen

Circle we drew
Guidance from past
We need it to last
So steady, not fast

Circle we built
Stone out of sand
Sprouts from the land
Raised by our hand.

Circle we blessed
Speaking to sky
Heart mind and eye
A soul that shall fly

Circle we are
When stone meets the sea
Continuity
Love; hope; family.

Practicing outdoors allows for people to gather together in spaces that help them connect to their faith a little more closely; a little more deeply. With that in mind, it seems natural to move onto talking about community. Community has become a bit of a key issue for me over the past couple of years. I used to feel like a bit of an island; I'm deeply introverted, and even when I found wonderful, kind groups of folks that enjoyed celebrating the seasons in similar ways to me, I still felt that we were a slightly larger island outside the "mainstream", struggling slightly to find our place in a wildly consumerist society.

Nowadays, I'm a member of several larger groups or communities that work together *across* various small islands like the ones I used to reside on (metaphorically speaking), helping them see that they're not alone, encouraging them to share their wisdom and knowledge where appropriate, and helping others forge connections to likeminded folks. From co-creating a four-continent spanning song to honour Hekate to holding a national online Earth Day festival, I've been lucky enough to be involved in some amazing community initiatives over the past few years.

Community: A body of persons of common and especially professional interests scattered through a larger society. (Merriam-Webster Dictionary)

Some definitions of community speak of locality or area. But the Pagan community is stronger because it spans so many areas. Thanks to the internet, Pagans and spiritual folks from all over the world can communicate and share ideas, without having to worry about the miles between them At no time has that been felt more deeply than during the chaos of 2020 and 2021, as the world hung in the grip of a pandemic which it little understood. During this time, it was more important than ever that we showed the members of our community that they weren't alone; that they could still connect to their spirituality and their faith, without putting themselves in danger.

One such endeavour was a huge online garden, encouraging

even those who were shielding and limited to the boundaries of their own homes to show us what they loved about the outdoors, nature, growing things, flowers, plants, even local wildlife. It was heartening to see that even during these difficult times, so many members of the community were still focused on living in eco-friendly ways. We saw toilet roll tubes used as potting tools; many a compost pile; wormariums; rescued animals – these ranged from horses to tiny bugs; kids watching the life cycles of caterpillars with endless fascination; upcycled plant pots; harvesting seeds for next season; plus, any number of crafty creations depicting deities, spirits, mandalas, and other ways of connecting with the divine.

Bringing the community together like this is more than just letting people know they aren't alone – although, of course, that's vital and absolutely crucial for mental health and wellbeing. Encouraging folks to share their simple ways of looking after the Earth inspires others to do the same. Often, people will go about their daily lives, gently and kindly, without considering that others may want to know how to live in such a way. By reaching out and asking those folks to share their lives and achievements with you and the wider community, you create a group-wide realisation that it's easy to do small actions that can make a big difference. Being told to do things is always a bit uncomfortable. Seeing others do things, thinking they're beautiful or useful or both, then wondering how to do those things yourself; that's how real change happens. That's the key to true inspiration.

Action: Think of a time you've been inspired to do something; anything at all, it doesn't have to be related to environmentalism or even your spirituality. What was it that inspired you? Why do you think it had this affect? If you can, write a few words about what the key was to really knowing this was something you wanted to do.

Building Your Community

Building your own community of likeminded people might be something you want to do, or you may want to find out how to join an existing community. Because Paganism and esoteric spiritualities are often considered mysterious or outside the mainstream, it can leave some folks feeling unsure as to how to get in touch with a particular organisation, or fearing that their query won't be welcomed. Towards the end of this book, there's a Useful Links section which has links to some organisations that may be useful if you want more information or would like to learn more about a particular organisation. Of course, you could start a whole new community, or sub-community, that caters to your specific interests or passions. This is an especially useful thing to do if you are trying to improve the local environment where you live, work, or study.

One example of a local community initiative is the community garden. This is where folks come together to turn a patch of land into a wonderful, green and growing space, filled with beautiful flowers, herbs, vegetables, fruits, or a combination thereof. At our most local park, there used to be spectacular flower displays running from spring into summer. Although these were beautiful, a couple of years ago a really stunning transformation took place. One of the larger beds which ran across the top of a hill, was suddenly half taken up with cabbages, carrot tops, tomatoes, beans, and nasturtiums. A local community group had gained permission to use the space to grow edible plants, with the proviso that anyone could come and help themselves. I won't lie; I cried a little when I saw this wonderful addition to our park. I've got a tear in my eye now; such kindness affects me deeply.

The knock-on effect goes further than providing food for the needy within our wider community. It shows folks that they can, absolutely, make a difference. It's inspiring and confidence building. For the folks that work on the garden, they get to connect to the Earth in a real and visceral way, the work can improve their fitness, and they'll surely associate that self-improvement with the Earth and the work they've done. Plus, for many, this might be their first instance of growing plants and learning about them, so in that way, it becomes a wonderful learning experience. Then there's purely practical points. For example, switching up what you grow in a particular area year on year discourages pests naturally, without the need for pesticides. Involving the community to pop by and weed reduces the need for herbicides (weedkiller). This stops unnecessary chemicals leaching into the soil and polluting waterways and killing local wildlife.

Setting up a community garden will be a different process depending upon where you live in the world, but here are some steps you might want to consider:

- Check if there already is one in your local area – research online or talk to community or local authority leaders.
- Who are you hoping to inspire? Think about who you will market the project towards – young or older? Unemployed folks? Specifically faith or spirituality based?
- Consider your land options. You might find a spare allotment for a small fee by searching online, or there might be some unused land you've got your eye on. Always check ownership and gain permission before you start digging. You might want to contact the Community Land Advisory Service for help and support here.
- Will this land have access to the right facilities? Think about accessibility for all, water, power for tools. I used to work on an allotment and it was wonderful but there was no electricity, so we had to invest in petrol-powered tools for some of the harder tasks. At that point, we has to wonder if that was ecologically sound.
- Plan your garden – what do you want to grow there?

Flowers? Vegetable? Or do you want to theme your garden? A Pagan garden could be themed by element, with red plants and flowers for fire, blue for water, green or brown for earth, and yellow and white for air. Or it might be plants associated with a particular deity, such as the many associated with Hekate; chamomile, garlic, and verbena, to name just a few. Or you may want to create a sensory garden, focusing on aroma, texture, colour, or even taste if you focus on edible plants.

- Always make sure you are aware of what plants are poisonous or irritants, and make sure your team of willing gardeners are aware of any allergies they may have and are medicated if need be. Antihistamines can be a life saver for the hay fever sufferer who loves gardening!

In North America, Wisconsin not-for-profit organisation The Community's Garden reports that this communal gardening is a growing phenomenon, as people realise how important it is to do their part to make the Earth a better place. They see gardening as a way to connect people to nature; something that seems, to me, inherently Pagan at its core. They talk about families reconnecting as they "unplug" from digital life and get their hands back into the soil; what better way to feel a deeper connection to the Earth *and* the community?

Other community initiatives might correlate more directly to pressing local concerns. Reducing pollution can be a real motivator to get people onside when it comes to environmental issues. Not everyone is an environmental scientist – nor can you expect them to be. But if you suggest that planting more trees in a local area could improve air quality or reduce the risk of flooding, then plenty of people are going to get on board with that. A cycle-to-work scheme that's directly linked to reducing respiratory issues or helping folks with asthma; that's going to have some real impact. Picking litter to improve a local beauty spot is going to be popular with many, especially those who use it regularly. People often respond to things better when they're framed in a relatable context. One of our local schools tried to raise awareness about how cars leaving their engines running outside the gates was problematic. They made a lot more headway with stubborn drivers when they talked about the direct correlation between traffic pollution and asthma in children. Vehicle fumes are an irritant and can trigger an asthma attack (Asthma UK, 2020), plus they can trigger allergies in those with hay fever or related conditions. Sometimes people struggle to see the bigger picture, and that's when it can be useful to bring environmental issues back to a local, relatable level, to help build the community you want.

We've talked a great deal about gathering together and working together to make sure those gatherings are environmentally sound and safe. Beyond this, there's so much more we can do when we work together as a community. Pagans, as you will no doubt understand, don't have a common faith or set of beliefs. There are literally hundreds of paths, often with very different cultural mindsets. Despite this, Pagans manage to come together in large numbers to make a difference when things matter. Organisations such as ones listed towards the end of this book help connect people, support them in any number of ways, and also give them channels to voice their opinions, concerns, fears, and hopes.

Action: The Pagan community was kind enough to lend me its collective ears when I was researching this book. I went out to the community and asked them three questions, and I'd like to ask you them now. You can write the answers in a journal, if you like, or simply think about them right now.

1.   What are the top three things you are concerned about in terms of the environment or the natural world?
2.   How does your Pagan path or spirituality connect to your

desire to protect the environment?

3. What specific actions do you take within your Pagan practice or spiritual endeavours that have a positive impact on either the local or wider environment?

Jot your answers somewhere, and keep those answers. They might become very useful keys in deciding what you do next in your journey towards a more environmentally kind lifestyle.

The multitude of answers I received was wide ranging but, reassuringly, very unified in that every single person who responded felt it was their responsibility to do something within their daily lives to make the world a better place, in some way.

Top Environmental Concerns for Pagans

Although I had hundreds of responses, these next few items rated as some of the top environmental concerns for members of the Pagan community.

- Pollution
- Habitat loss and species extinction
- Climate change

I find it absolutely no coincidence at all that, according to various different sources across the world, these three items rank in the top environmental issues facing our planet today. It seems our spiritual community is pretty clued up when it comes to what's important.

Pollution includes air pollution which we've touched on a few times, water pollution, soil pollution including the loss of nutrients in soil, and other problems such as waste management.

Habitat loss leads to species extinction. Deforestation is a major problem, because around 80% of land-based life lives in the forests (United Nations, 2020). Forests currently absorb around two billion tonnes of carbon each year, a number which will only drop every time more forests are destroyed. Forests are also absolutely essential to human life. Trees literally provide the air we breathe, plus they provide any number of natural resources from wood to medicine. We have to find ways of sustaining our forests, to stop our own decline as well as the disappearance of numerous species.

You can help protect forests, by checking the products you buy. Look out for the FSC label on any of your paper or wood products, including facial and toilet tissues, paper towels, and even furniture. FSC is the badge of the Forest Stewardship Council and is a little cartoon tree with a tick coming off it. Buying items with this badge on ensures the wood comes from managed forests, where the number of trees cut down is strictly limited, pesticides are used as responsibly as possible, and the rights of indigenous peoples are protected.

The Karipuna People are a prime example of when deforestation becomes more than just an abstract, environmental concern. The Karipuna live in the Brazilian Amazon rainforest, right up against the Bolivian border. Their village of Panorama nestles in the forest, by the river, which they use for food, transport, hygiene, and leisure. There are less than 60 Karipuna, and they rely on the Amazon completely. That means that those wishing to claim these lush stretches of forest for logging or clearing are putting the Karipuna at very real risk of extinction.

The Amazon is cleared for a number of reasons; land to graze animals, agricultural land for crops such as soy, mining resources like minerals, or simply for the wood. Although the Karipuna's land is technically protected by Brazilian law, illegal land-grabbing and deforestation is a real problem. Leader Adriano Karipuna has addressed the United Nations, appealing to the international community to fight organised crime and protect Indigenous Peoples who cannot survive if the forest keeps being cleared.

The good news is that the Karipuna are managing to reclaim

some of their lost land, thanks to high-tech forest monitoring systems and an intricate knowledge of the legal rights that protect them. However, this is just one tiny snapshot of the struggles indigenous peoples all over the globe face, thanks to irresponsible resource management and the insistence on progress at any cost. Protecting these people means protecting the lands and forests they live in, which in turn protects the planet itself. Once we begin to understand this, the term *global community* really starts to make sense.

What can you do? Be aware of where your food comes from. Soya or soy is particularly problematic. It's a common protein source, especially for vegetarians or vegans or those trying to reduce their meat intake. It's also used as feed for animals bred for meat – around 90% of all soya grown globally ends up as animal feed (Greenpeace, 2020). Huge swathes of forest are cut down to provide land to grow soya on. Since 2006, agreements have been in place to protect the Amazon from further clearing for soya production, but other forests and fragile biomes are now at risk including the Gran Chaco and the Brazilian Cerrado. As well as destroying habitats and removing the trees that we so desperately need to absorb the carbon we keep pumping into the atmosphere, the growth of soya often involves the use of literally tons of pesticides which kills or harms native animals and pollutes waterways.

You can buy soy or soya (they are the same product, but you may see both names used in ingredients lists) sustainably by looking out for the Round Table on Responsible Soy (RTRS) certificate on the products you buy. If you buy meat, do a little research on the store you buy from. It's recently come to light that many major UK supermarkets and some fast-food giants are stocking chicken which is fed on soya linked to intense deforestation and out of control forest fires (Bureau of Investigative Journalism, 2020). The American company which exports the soya insists no laws have been broken, which is problematic both on a moral and environmental level. When big businesses won't stop doing something that's damaging because it makes money and it's not illegal, that's a moral problem. When consumers don't know they're buying food that's linked to industrial deforestation, that's an environmental issue. What we can do, as consumers, is keep up to date with the news, look for the RTRS badge where possible, and even ask stores and suppliers about the products they make. When we choose to spend our money with companies making the effort to behave more ethically, that *has* to have a positive impact spiritually as well. Plus, if you raise awareness about any issues with food, food production, or other environmental issues, you're supporting and helping your community, too. Just always remember to fact check and get your information from credible sources.

How Pagans in the Community Connect
Spirituality to Environmentalism

As I said earlier, I was privileged to chat with various members of our wider community about what they felt environmentalism meant to them, but also about how they personally connected their own brand of spirituality to either their local environment or the health of the planet in general. Some of the answers were absolutely fascinating, and I was delighted to learn that plenty of modern Pagans and spiritual folks still find traditional ways of doing daily tasks, in order to specifically connect with the world around them or be kinder to the environment.

Spiritually, many folks on a nature-based path felt that they could expand their reverence for trees by working voluntarily with organisations such as the Woodland Trust. Others spoke about how by protecting nature and the environment, we are protecting ourselves and our own home. There were comments that we need to learn to appreciate what we have because humans might die out, but eventually the world will heal and carry on without us if we are not careful. In other words, the Earth may be here long after us, but right now the harm we are doing is as much to ourselves as to the planet.

One animist commented that they felt like they were creating a community with the hills, the sea, and the trees and by that, focusing on the life-web in which they were connected with Mother Earth. I relate to this a great deal. I am only a trainee Druid, but I have embraced animism almost instinctively my whole life. Everything has its own life or spirit to me, and while I know not everyone sees the world like this, we can surely all accept that every plant, rock, insect or grain of sand has a crucial role in our increasingly fragile ecosystems.

Most Pagans I spoke to noted that their spirituality was intrinsically intertwined with nature, whether that was via honouring the earth as a whole or a specific reverence for trees, animals, or other aspects of our environment. Many were actively seeking ways to make a positive difference in the world, or trying to live sacred reciprocity with all the life in the world and the world itself. Some of the ways they do this include:

- Reusing and upcycling rather than buying new (see Chapter 2).
- Using mechanical rather than electric or fossil-fuel powered tools, for example, cutting grass with a scythe.
- Becoming more self-sufficient by growing or foraging for their own food, and by growing other useful resources such as grass to cut for hay for livestock, or medicinal herbs.
- Gathering and recycling trash into tools like baskets.
- Carving spiritual tools such as wands, staves, or figurines out of discarded wood like fenceposts.
- Harvesting responsibly, being sure to leave habitats for wildlife.
- Making household items like soap and detergent, the added benefit of this being you know exactly what's

going into it and for those with a magical bent, you can boost the power of your cleaners with some essential oils or spell work.

- Buying and replacing large appliances as infrequently as possible.
- Buying second hand as much as possible.
- When buying new, buying items that are built to last.
- Buying goods with less packaging.
- Avoiding single use items, particularly plastics.
- Checking that products are produced in an environmentally conscious way before purchasing.
- Cutting out or reducing driving or air travel.
- Voting for political parties or individuals whose policies protect the Earth.
- Looking after their own land with biodiversity in mind; preserving wildflower meadows, grazing animals carefully, housing animals in buildings made from recycled farm waste.
- Generating their own electricity.
- Sourcing water from boreholes.
- Buying local and supporting and promoting local businesses.
- No-dig vegetable beds, which may protect the biodiversity of the soil beneath.
- Taking a job that reflects this love for the planet, such as ecologist or conservationist.
- Leading workshops or inspiring others to care more deeply for the planet.
- Composting.
- Feeding the birds.
- Planting trees.
- Foraging.
- Volunteering or working for animal welfare organisations.
- Moving away from fossil fuels, for example, by driving

an electric car
- Create wild areas in gardens or parks (where possible) to encourage biodiversity
- Carry tenets like *do no harm* over to the world we live in.

This last point has become a reality for many vegan members of our community. They have cut animal products out of their lifestyle, both to protect these animals as their spirituality demands, but also, as I discussed with various folks, to protect the environment. I've only recently become aware of the damage the meat industry is doing to the environment. Fossil fuels are by far the greatest producer of greenhouse gas emissions, but agriculture is a huge contender, accounting for 10% of all greenhouse gases, in America at least (EPA, 2018). One of the major contributors to the agricultural emissions is livestock, specifically their digestive gases, which account for at least 25% of agricultural emissions. Producing feed for livestock also adds to the total emissions, as does dealing with the animal waste like manure.

I don't feel hugely qualified to extoll the virtues of veganism because I'm not vegan myself, and want to avoid hypocrisy. But, it's clear to me that at least reducing the amount of meat and dairy we eat will have a massive impact on improving the environment. Of course, it's important to look out for traps like eating a diet focused around damaging crops like soya, but it is absolutely possible to have a plant-based and ethical diet. We eat much less meat than we used to, and I adore exploring plant-based recipes – particularly spicy food! Chick pea curries, dahl made with red or brown lentils, and a range of tangy stir-fry style dishes are all favourites in my house now. We have a local supplier that makes veggie burgers and sausages out of plants like beets, carrots, peas and more- no soya in sight. I've made my own immensely popular veggie burgers with simply crushed beans, chillies, and spices like cumin and coriander. Creativity is the key, I find, when expanding into the world of plant-based meals.

The most exciting thing about the list of actions Pagans are taking is how readily that information was shared. The chance to share their achievements, hopes, and dreams with the wider community was one that most folks grasped eagerly, and conversations started between many, increasing the connections and growing the sense of community even more.

A final point of action that came up again and again was this: We should pass on our knowledge and passion for protecting the Earth to the next generation. I completely agree with that sentiment, so let's explore that in the next chapter.

Chapter Nine

Raising the Next Generation

I'm going to start this chapter with this excerpt from one of my blogs, from Imbolc 2020:

It snowed for the first time today; the first time this winter, anyway. The nine-year-old was shrieking, "Mummy, it's snowing! It's snowing! It's a sign that the rest of the day is going to be good."
Because although snow can mean disruption and even danger, for a nine-year-old with none of these adult concerns, it's simply beautiful and fun.

I love that he sees omens like this in the simplest things. A heavy rainfall prompts him to sit at the front door, wrapped in blankets, listening to the song of the rain. A crow is a guardian. Three crows is the Morrigan- yeah, he can't listen to me tell him to brush his teeth but he overhears my spiritual work and stores it all away! I don't mind. I like that he sees the stories and symbols in these things. Whether it becomes part of his own spirituality or religion, that can wait until later, or whenever he wants.

Imbolc is a strange, transitional time. It's buried under snow or frozen in frost, but greenery is peeking through. Spring is starting to make a go of it. Brigid is the goddess we honour at this time, associated with smithing and crafting, song, poetry, and family. How does my nine year old relate to this?

He's writing. He waxes lyrical about the glowing sunrises, now at getting up time instead of just after. He gawks at the stormy wind; the ridiculous rain; the frigid frosts giving way to sudden sunshine. And he builds. He makes a parachute, ties string and wraps tape and colours and paints and draws. His creativity bursts out in buds of new growth, just like the first golden crocuses showing their faces by his school.

I take note, because it's easy, as a grown up, to forget these small pleasures. I lose myself in his wonder at a windy day, and pray to my gods and goddesses that I always carry a spark of that wonder with me. (First published on the Pagan Federation Community Support Team Blog, February 2020.)

Kids are our greatest teachers when it comes to appreciating the world around us. Anyone who has children or has the chance to interact with children will know that there is nothing more magical than seeing them become enthralled with nature. That look of amazement when they see leaves fall, or dragonflies zoom past, or even midge larvae in a murky pool of water. Whenever you see that wonder in action, so whatever you can to encourage it. I know it can be tricky when your youngest wants to make friends with a slug and it makes you feel nauseous, but that kindness towards living things could be the start of a reverence for nature that will stick with them their entire lives.

Whether you decide to deliberately raise your children on a Pagan path or not, the simple truth is you can't go wrong by teaching them how to look after the environment around them. Our children are the first generation growing up fully aware of the damage previous generations have done to the world. They will learn that the Earth is being ravaged by the effects of climate change, thanks to the actions of former generations, and the lack of action by current the generation, in some cases. Regardless of whether we, as individuals, contributed towards the problems, collectively as a society we all have a responsibility to pick up the slack. It's tragic that we are inevitably leaving so much of this hard work on our children's shoulders, but at least we can give them the tools to best navigate their way through this world with as little negative impact on the environment as possible. I think the first step in this is to foster that spark of love for the natural world around us, whether that's glorious woodlands or a patch of moss on a city wall.

Lead by Example

I guess this is good advice for any aspect of parenting. Kids do what they see, not what they're told. Okay, sometimes they do what they're told! But they watch us, they memorise the things we do, and they will definitely repeat or imitate it at some point. That's how they learn to walk and talk; it's how they learn to treat others kindly; it is the primary way they will learn what the best way is to treat the world around them.

Let your kids watch you sort the rubbish out. If you split it into recycling, see if they want to help. Go at the task with enthusiasm, and they might want to join in without too much prompting. My three-year-old is obsessed with putting one thing in another at the moment, which is great for tidying up. We talk about everything: "Where do the bottles go?" "Where's the bin, can you find the bin?" and we make a game out of everything.

If getting your kids involved in what they might see as "boring housework" is just too difficult (I understand, believe me, I do), then lead by example in smaller ways. Let them watch you upcycle, or sew up a rip in some trousers instead of throwing them away. Make sure they're watching as you carefully dispose of litter properly when out and about. Talk about why you turn the lights off as you leave a room, or why we turn the tap off while we brush our teeth. All these tiny, daily rituals become strokes in a bigger picture as they grow up and absorb not just what you say, but what you do.

In the Garden

If you have a garden, even if it's only tiny, this is a wonderful starting point for getting your kids interested in nature. According to the National Geographic, you're just as likely to discover a new species in your garden as in a tropical rainforest (Mueller, 2014); how exciting is that?!? Taking photos of the plants, bugs, birds, and other creatures in your yard can become a fascinating project; not just a fun exploration but intensely educational on many levels. Kids learn about biodiversity, and enjoy the surprise factor of just how many species can survive right there in their yard. They learn that lifting a stone gently can reveal a home for tiny families, different to their yet similar in many respects. They learn about being gentle in order to preserve these creatures and their habitats; a gentleness which, if nurtured, could stay with them their entire lives.

If you don't have a garden or yard, you could grow some plants on a windowsill, or try making a terrarium. You could learn how to craft a bird box or bat box, and involve your children in that project. You might have somewhere to hang a basket of flowers, or trailing fruit like strawberries or some species of raspberry or tomato. Watch for pests like aphids, then watch for their predators like ladybirds, and explain what's happening and why. Explain why, thanks to the ladybird, you don't have to use harmful chemicals like pesticides. Plant flowers that attract bees, and talk about pollination and how as well as pollinating the flowers, the bees also pollinate our food crops, so looking after them is looking after ourselves. This can start conversations about how everything is connected, and the beginnings of an understanding of ecosystems.

You can even insert some aspects of your own spirituality into your garden ecology. Talk about the turn of the seasons and how that relates to your faith. Speak of plants and trees and which deities or beings they're connected to. Tell stories, share folklore and superstitions, and show how looking after the things we hold sacred is about looking after the planet itself.

Nature Journeys

As and when you can, taking your kids out into nature to find out what's in the wider world is the next step in making them fall in love with the world. Think about all the different settings you could take them to. You can think as big and as small as you like, depending on where you are in the world. Here are a selection of outdoor settings where you can find nature, even in surprising places:

- A city street – think moss and lichen, birds, city trees, rats, bugs
- Deserts
- Forests and woodland
- A local stream or beck
- Rivers
- The seashore
- A patch of grass in a housing estate
- Fields
- Hedgerows
- Farms – look out for ones that encourage visitors
- Grass verges
- Mountains
- Lakes
- Sand dunes
- Limestone pavement – a stunning, natural formation
- Cliffs
- Moors
- Parks
- Flower gardens
- Stately homes or other places of national interest

Can you think of any others? I'm sure I've only scratched the surface here. If there is one recommendation I could give, it's to always take photos whenever you visit anywhere with your kids; of them, and of the nature you find. I adore looking back on photos of my eldest and the adventures we went on when he was younger. We went rock climbing on Ilkley Moor (Yorkshire, UK) when he was about six years old, and I have a favourite picture of him sitting astride one of the rocks, triumphant. That same day, we saw butterflies and any number of delicate wildflowers hidden among the grasses of the moor. Having a record of that is a snapshot of pure happiness, plus a reminder of how easy it is to reconnect to nature when you have a child with you.

Listen

Listening to your kids is absolutely key, especially if you want to nurture a sense of kindness and thoughtfulness in them. It's also a great way to encourage them to listen to you – something every parent wants! My 3-year-old calls me out on this all the time. Sometimes I'll drift off when she's babbling, distracted by a work email or something similar, and she shouts, "Mummy! Talk to me!" in tones that brook no disobedience. I immediately apologise, and put my phone down and listen intently. I want her to know that she's important, and that every word from her is a gift. With the older ones, it's sometimes more of a challenge, especially when they spend twenty minutes explaining the intricacies of a particular Fortnite Battle Lab strategy, but I do make the effort.

Why is this so important in terms of encouraging kids to be kinder to the environment? Well, firstly, a dialogue involves both parties listening as well as talking, and if you're completely engaged with your kids and what they say, there's more chance they will take on board what they say to you. Being in tune with everything they say also allows you to listen out for cues and questions that become learning opportunities. "Why" is a powerful question, and one you will probably hear all the time. Be prepared to answer questions about your spirituality in an age-appropriate way, questions about why you do the things you do, like upcycling, recycling, witching the lights off, saving water, and watch out for your kids naturally showing an interest in nature so you can start conversations about it.

You might discover, quite by accident, that your child has a fascination for trees, or flowers, or even for looking for shapes in the clouds. These are all opportunities to talk about how important these things are – not necessarily in a super serious way, but perhaps in a light-hearted, conversational way. Absorb what your kids tell you, even if half of it seems completely irrelevant, as it might surprise you later down the line just how much they've absorbed from you, too.

Reward Curiosity

Kids are naturally curious, and rewarding that curiosity goes a long way towards ensuring it doesn't disappear as they get older. Curiosity is the root of science, and scientists, including conservationists and environmental experts, and who we need to help us understand exactly what we need to do to fix the problems the world is facing. Spirituality and kindness are what we need in order to understand and appreciate *why* we have to make those changes. Curiosity can lead to both scientific and spiritual discoveries, so nurturing it is an absolute win-win.

I'm currently involved in a scheme called the Aether Patches, run by the Pagan Federation. I came on board a little after its conception, and was absolutely delighted by the idea: a range of quests, all based around the five primary senses – smell, touch, taste, sight, and hearing – encouraging curiosity and spirituality in kids of all ages. Upon completion of quests, children can get a beautiful, embroidered patch to show their achievement. The advantage of schemes like this is that they help build communities, and allow parents, carers and kids to talk about their faith and their experiences openly and easily. It also allows the child to keep a tactile record of their learning, their achievements, and expand upon the different ways in which they interact with the world and their faith or spirituality.

You could also do more ad hoc rewards. A good idea is to relate rewards directly to action, for example, if a kid suddenly shows interest in sharks, you could take them to an aquarium to learn more – a fun day out, and a learning experience. Do check that the aquarium you visit is dedicated to conservation rather than entertainment. One particular animal centre we love is a home to rescued animals that are either being rehabilitated for release, or too badly injured or used to human contact to return to the wild. We feel good about spending our money here, because we know the money goes right back into animal rescue and educating the public on how to better protect the life around our seashores. They have whole rooms dedicate to education, with tactile and interactive resources where kids can look at cross sections of habitats, solve puzzles, and learn about the dangers of litter and pollution.

Nurturing Spirituality

If you do decide to involve your kids on your particular spiritual or religious path, then there are various ways that you can do this which also encourage their devotion towards nature and the natural world. Seasonal festivities are a great way to start with this. By working through the wheel of the year and highlighting the festivals appropriate to your path, you're teaching your kids about the turn of the seasons as it relates to your part of the world. You could start by simply pointing out the differences in weather at each time of year; pointing out when the baby animals are starting to appear in springtime; watching out for birds nesting and highlighting when the green leaf buds start to appear on the trees. Something as simple as talking about how it gets warmer and colder throughout the year is not just great for science and education; it helps kids feel in tune with the seasons and begin to feel that connection to the Earth as it turns and changes.

You can't help but feel a little bit protective towards something you're strongly connected to. Starting our kids off with that feeling at a young age, I think, inevitably leads to a sense of responsibility over the planet. As your kids get older, you could make a place within your rituals for them, perhaps simply to say a little bit about what they love about the particular festival or season you're celebrating. If ritual is not your thing, or if you wouldn't be comfortable including your kids in yours, then there are other ways to involve them in seasonal festivities. To be honest, I don't involve my kids in ritual at all. This isn't because I don't think it's suitable, but I want them to make their own minds up about their faith and spirituality. I talk about mine openly, and they show a lot of interest. But we celebrate the turns of the wheel in other ways; with food, crafts, planting seeds, telling stories, and sharing gifts. You could simply talk about what's happening in your part of the world at this time of year. You could take a trip away with likeminded folks. We usually go camping at Autumn Equinox, and the kids run feral (safely) and catch up and tell ghost stories, but they also watch the curlews flying high above, and the rabbits in the hedgerows, and listen out for the owls at night whilst sat round the fire.

2020's Autumn Equinox was a little different due to the pandemic situation. Me, my husband, and my son sat around the fire pit in the garden, sharing hot chocolate with marshmallows. It was the first noticeably colder night since the summer holidays, chilly even though it was only September. We continued the tradition of telling stories, sharing those which meant something to each of us. My son told stories about urban legends and cryptids; something he's really into at the moment. I told tales of Celtic myths, like about the god Lugh and his many skills. We shared snippets of folklore and traditions, and we connected over those, all the time appreciating the turn of the season, noticing how it was getting colder; noticing the warmer surrounding days, even though the leaves were already starting to turn; noticing the birds were starting to roost a little earlier of an evening; noticing the agile swifts, our summer visitors, were getting ready to leave for the winter.

Animals

Watching the behaviour and habits of animals other than humans, like the swifts that come and go, is a great way to understand how something can be completely in tune with the turning of the seasons. Getting kids involved with animals is generally very easy, because most kids naturally gravitate towards anything that is cute, interesting or smaller than them. That's why so many children love looking after smaller children, or become fiercely protective of younger siblings – even when they might seem like they hate them, some of the time! That nurturing instinct seems to spill over onto animals – in my experience, anyway. Look for ways to expand that instinct into a curiosity about animals in general and the natural world. One resource is, of course, the internet. There are many fact sheets and articles online about just about any animal. Just be sure to fact check before sharing online facts with your child, as literally anyone can say they are an expert online. Another media resource is the television, with many streaming services offering fantastic documentaries about wildlife, ecology, the environment and more.

You might even find that there are local events encouraging kids to get involved with animals. One of our local pet stores put on several workshops during the summer holidays, allowing children to come and see different types of animals, learn about them, their natural habitats, how to look after them and how to respect them. I was really impressed with the focus on animal welfare, and was happy to discover that the pet store in question promoted rescue animals finding homes, and refused to sell animals to anyone they felt wouldn't be a responsible pet owner – hard to realistically monitor, I guess, but lovely to see that they were trying. Having a pet is a huge commitment and I think kids who get pets should know exactly how to look after it. Teaching kids about what animals need whilst they are young and encouraging them to put this into action fosters the idea that animals are as worthy of respect as human beings. If a child learns to respect an animal hey have as a pet, hopefully that feeling of respect will spill over onto all animals, especially if their curiosity leads them to learn more about a variety of animals, both domestic and wild. Just remember to temper that curiosity with caution to avoid bites and scratches. Another way to connect animals to spirituality and paganism is to look at the correspondences and folklore attached to favourite animals. Crows are nature's cleaners, scavenging for rotten meat and other "delicacies". Perhaps you could teach your child about their connection to particular deities, or traditional tales about the crow. This is particularly poignant if you can find animals that are local to your area and create some magic around them with the aid of stories and myth. Explore your faith, find the significant animals, and see if any are close to you. If not, perhaps there's a way you could visit them, or even watch a documentary about them. Understanding the other living things in our faith helps us stay connected in a deeper way, and refreshed that yearning to keep the planet we *all* live on safe and well.

Action: Start a nature diary with your little ones. Have a book, notepad, or even a digital app (I use the notes app on my phone) and log every time you see something interesting. This could be a bird in the garden, a butterfly outside the window, or even clouds making unusual or familiar shapes. Notice which entries make your child most excited. Whatever it is, try and make sure they get more of that in their lives. If they got giddy about seeing a fox, watch a documentary about foxes with them or get a book out of the library about foxes. Feed that sense of wonder, in the hope that it stays with them as they grow up. You could print out photos and keep a scrapbook, or teach your child how to use a computer to keep their own record as they get older. This could lead to them becoming interested in preserving their habitats, perhaps in your local area, or the wider community. Or it might foster a desire to watch and learn more about a particular species, nurturing the scientist within.

If we carefully feed fuel to the sparks of passion we see in our children now when it comes to nature, animals, and the outdoors, we could be raising the next generation of true conservationists and the most intelligent and effective environmentalists the world has ever seen.

Chapter Ten

The Big Picture

Parakeets on the banks
Of the cold, cold river
We sit and bake
Listen to them scream
Flashes of green
Echoing the duck weed
Yet the ducks hide
Not wishing to be fried
We watch them dream
And listen to the parakeets
Scream

While over in Spain
Manure explodes
Intro raging wildfires
Exposing the BS
In the most literal way

While over in France
Folks collapse and gasp
Even die, even dying
Whilst wondering why

While we sip margaritas
Dip toes in the ooze
Of the cold, cold river
Watching green streaks
Speed of sound
Tree to tree

Free to go where they will

Lovely summer
But listen
To the screams.

I wrote this rather bleak and dramatic poem in June of 2019, when there genuinely were piles of exploding manure and folks collapsing and dying from the heat in Europe. I was at an early summer fair at a marina near my home, sat by the cool water. I was watching parakeets in wonder, as they are not native to my part of the world but they have made it their own, as it's now warm enough for them to survive there. Is it okay to be happy about the arrival of these beautiful green birds, while people die just a few hundred miles to the south?

There are no easy answers, but hopefully, throughout this book, you've found a few changes you could make within your own life and spiritual practice to help make the world a better place. If we all work together, we could see less rubbish in landfill. Less pressure on recycling plants. A lower carbon footprint as we buy more things as locally as possible. More nutritious soil thank to clever composting and turning a blind eye to the odd weed or wild patch. But, why is it so important, now more than ever?

Climate Change

I've already touched on the climate change crisis and its affects earlier in this book, such as wilder and longer lasting storms, or even the seasonal timings beginning to change in some parts of the world. There may be some debate over the seriousness of climate change, but scientists agree that potential effect include:

- More severe and frequent wildfires.
- More frequent and severe tropical storms, which last for

longer.
- Increased risk of drought in some areas.
- Increased risk of flooding in others.

The average temperature of our beautiful planet has increased 2 degrees Fahrenheit during the 20th century (NASA, 2020). As an average, that's a huge difference. Of course, local temperatures fluctuate all the time. It's important to remember that this is the Earth *as a whole*. Even the coldest places are now 2 degrees warmer than they were 120 years ago, at the time of writing this book. The Intergovernmental Panel on Climate Change (IPCC) predicts that in the next century, the global average will increase anywhere between 2.5 and 10 degrees. This might mean longer growing seasons for some, particularly in the Western United States. However, it will also lead to some very wet winters and springs, countered by intense droughts and heatwaves in the warmer months. NASA reports that by the end of the 21st century, what would be classed as a one-in-twenty-year heatwave will occur every two to three years, instead. Hurricanes will continue to increase in strength and duration, and destructive potential. Plus, the sea levels could rise by up to 8 feet as land ice continues to melt.

During 2020, scientists from Ohio State University reported a significant and scary point of no return. The Greenland ice sheet, the largest ice mass on the planet after Antarctica, has declined to such a point that even if global warming were to cease *right now*, the ice may never be replenished. The ice will continue to melt, contributing at least a millimetre per year to sea levels. That might not sound a lot, but when you realise that's irreversible, and also combine it with other melting ice masses on the planet, that's a swiftly rising sea level. This is not an observation that's sprung out of nowhere; 40 years of research and satellite images led into this phenomenal study, allowing researchers to place some confident predictions (King et al, 2020). Bear in mind, these findings apply in the case of no further global warming. Which, sadly, is not the case.

So, realistically, what can we do? What can *you* do? How can you put your earth-based spirituality into action to make a real difference? Thankfully, small actions do make a difference. That's because there are 7.8 billion of us and counting. Follow the tips in this book, practice your spirituality and go about your daily lives in a sustainable and kind way, but you may want to go further.

I think some Pagans and spiritual folks may avoid intense environmental activism because they may be concerned that their practice may become too political. It's easy to get bogged down in politics, which as we all know can be extremely divisive – a reason why many try to avoid it.

However, I think it's important to remember that, as I said in the introduction to this book, environmentalism *shouldn't* be political as we all need to live here, regardless of our beliefs. Sadly, green issues often become political issues, because of the policies that certain ruling bodies and governments put into place. Forests and ancient woodlands go unprotected from the relentless plod of "progress". Our immense and beautiful oceans slowly fill with plastic while corporations who are the prime culprits in many cases receive tax breaks. Other companies fail to follow basic ethical practices while politicians turn a blind eye.

I'm not here to judge or make outspoken political statements. I'm not qualified to do so. But I would hope that anybody who is following a spiritual path that is somehow involved in the care of our Earth would *always* look to those in power to see how they are treating the planet. This might mean governments, corporations, local leaders, or even leaders of community organisations. I find a good litmus test for any organisation is to see how they treat the world around them – and how they encourage others to do the same.

Using Your Power

Regardless of your views on magic or other supernatural forces, hopefully, you have at least two forms of power. One is you can vote, or if you're not old enough yet, you soon will be able to. Use this vote wisely. The second power you can wield is your money. We live in a mostly capitalist society. Where you spend your money has *enormous* power. If we all stop spending with corrupt corporations or businesses that won't listen and do better, those businesses will eventually cease to exist. Look up the companies you love. So, do their ethics sit well with your own? Are they producing sustainably? I'm not here to name and shame companies, but there are certainly plenty of resources out there for anyone looking to shop with a more ethical mindset.

Even if you don't have spare cash to spend with companies who are supporting environmental causes or ethical production, you can exercise power in other ways. Share their advertisements. Review previous products from them. Leave comments on their social media. Your voice is more powerful than you know, and it's a powerful form of magic to use your voice as a catalyst for change.

As I said, this book is not the place for political or social debate. I'm not here to tell you who to vote for or who to buy with, as my views on that could fill a whole different book! Come visit me on social media for that type of debate.

How you use your power is entirely down to you and your own personal ethics. Choosing leaders or local politicians is about weighing up everything that's going on in your life and the lives of those you care about, against the policies on offer, and also seeing how those policies will affect disadvantaged folks. You never know when something might happen to leave you in a worse position than you are right now, so always vote for those who will help get you back on your feet should that happen.

I would always suggest you take a look at the green policies on offer. Does this party or organisation support the reduction of greenhouse emissions and other environmental impacts? Or, if you're looking at a company, are their products ethically sourced and sustainable? These are the types of questions we need to start asking as a matter of course. It should no longer be a chore to get this information, as companies should be transparent and providing these facts upfront.

The fashion industry is a surprising example of action being taken to do the right thing for the environment. There is now a scheme to reduce the use of hazardous chemicals to zero during the manufacture of clothes and fabrics: The Zero Discharge of Hazardous Chemicals campaign which is working towards an industry standard of safer chemistry. Some really big fashion names have joined up, but again, you have to do a little research to find out who is certified to say they are a part of the scheme.

This might not seem like an inherently Pagan topic, but at the end of day we all wear clothes (sometimes!), so when you're buying clothes it's so helpful to see a certification on the label that reassures you that the materials used to make it were sustainable and ethically sourced. Wouldn't it also be amazing to know that during the process of making the item of clothing, local waterways were kept clean and hopefully the air was not polluted? Or, perhaps, that any emissions were offset in some way? Look out for these certifications when buying a beautiful rug for your yoga room or your healing area, or the stunning robes that you need for ritual purposes, or special scarfs, bags, or boxes to keep your tarot cards or runes in.

We all purchase *things*, some of us only from time to time, and some of us more frequently. Not everything is handmade or locally sourced. That's why it's so vital that companies improve and clearly label their products to show us exactly how they're being made and where the source materials are coming from. This makes it easier for us, as consumers, to make the ethical choice. We can put pressure on companies to do just that, by only buying from the companies that are completely transparent and ethical. That's our power as a consumer, and should never be underrated! I'm not the biggest fan of capitalism as a concept but there are ways to work within the system to make change. My triple whammy is:

- Research
- Vote
- Spend wisely

I don't always get it right. I'm not sure anyone does. Sometimes it feels like an impossible task to filter out the facts from the propaganda and (I loathe this phrase) "fake news" circling social media. Like most people, I do the best I can. If even £100 of my income per year is spent with a company that is proud to make ethical choices rather than one that doesn't, then that's a success to me. If I can inspire even one person to do the same, then that's doubled that success – or even more if they go on to be that inspiration for others.

Pagan Activists

If you are interested in more actively making a difference within the systems that we're all in, there are a number of ways of doing this. There are plenty of organisations that you can become involved with who attempt to directly influence a range of organisations from businesses to government, with the goal of forcing them to make them make better choices when it comes to environmental decisions. A prime example of this is Extinction Rebellion (XR). XR focuses on raising awareness of the "unprecedented global emergency" we are currently facing. They believe, based on science, that we are witnessing a mass extinction event right now due to climate breakdown.

In October of 2020, XR members took part in the Autumn

Uprising, a series of protests and acts of non-violent civil disobedience designed to raise awareness of the "criminal inactivity" of governments and corporations in dealing with climate change.

Not everyone agrees with the methods these organisations take. Sir David Attenborough went on record as saying that while he believed you could *not* be too radical in the right against climate change, one could not start breaking the law. XR responded with a literal olive branch and a hope that dialogue could be opened so that Sir David might start to appreciate and support their methods more (Menendez, 2020). Sometimes the actions of activists can be seen as overtly political, or simple shock tactics for attention for the organisation, rather than the cause. I tend to disagree. I think that a little bit of shock is what is needed, in some cases, to get the message through.

Currently, there are activists trying to stop a new highspeed railway being built. This railway, called HS2, is designed to connect the north and south of England, but for many, it feels completely unnecessary and a horrible waste of resources. The worst thing about it is, in my opinion, that HS2 is cutting through swathes of ancient British woodland. Every time I think about the callous culling of ancient trees and all the things that live on and in them, my eyes well up with tears. The organisation behind HS2 promised to plant 7 million trees to mitigate the ecological damage, which makes no sense in terms of the irreplaceable habitats and ecosystems that have grown up over hundreds of years. So far, 234,000 trees have been planted, and already, 89,000 of those new trees have died. Authorities decided that it was easier and more cost-effective to replace them than to keep watering them during the hot summer of 2018 (Sharman, 2019).

Activists have been trying to block the work being carried out. Some activists created rope walkways across the trees and stayed up there for hours. Contractors at the Denham Country Park site, just outside of London, cut some of the ropes and the activists fell, one of them ending up in hospital (Courtney-Guy, 2020). Despite this, it was the protestors that ended up in court, rather than the HS2 team. Hardly seems right, does it?

Of course, strapping yourself to trees or gluing yourself to pavements isn't the only way to make a difference; not by a long way. If you feel uncomfortable with the idea of civil disobedience, there are plenty of other ways you can become an activist without breaking the law. Groups like Pagan Aid support a wide range of environmental causes as well as fighting poverty, and often put the call out for volunteers to help in a variety of roles. Pagan Aid aims to "help people meet their basic needs through living in harmony with nature." That includes promoting permaculture, helping hurricane victims, and promoting sustainable development, just to scratch the surface.

You can look out for groups on social media that promote some form of eco-paganism: combining spiritual paths with active ways to look after the Earth. As well as joining these groups and participating in discussions, you could offer to do some administration for them, manage or respond to comments or messages, or even engage members in discussions about what they would like to get out of being in these groups. Most roles like this only take up an hour of your time each week, or just a few minutes here and there. As groups expand, that workload might intensify, but there are usually more people willing to get on board and help by the time a group reaches this level.

You could take content from these groups or organisations and share it on your own social media channels with links back to the original groups. This seems like such a simple thing to do, but it can actually be extraordinarily effective. It's a way of getting an environmental message out to a wider audience. If even one of your contacts likes or shares that photo, the message gets an even wider audience, which can then have a snowball effect. If a single person who interacts with a photo about, say, recycling, changes one habit for the better, that's you managing to make the world a better place. Tiny changes shared among millions of people add up to a massive impact, especially when you consider that over the period of a few years, a small change every day amounts to a very big change indeed. In 2020, there were nearly 5 billion people with access to a computer (IWS, 2020). That's a whole lot of opportunity to influence positive change.

Staying Motivated

Sometimes it can be really hard to stay motivated. Occasionally, you might stop to take a look around, and all you can see is people failing to recycle and throwing their litter on the ground, or people being callous with the environment, or even just mocking the idea of climate change being as big a problem as it is. We're almost at the point of no return; when you feel like the only person who wants to make a difference, how can you stay motivated to carry on that fight?

The important first step is to avoid guilt or self-recrimination. This can be hard, especially when you *need* to use plastic, single-use items, or take multiple trips in the car. But we all have our own individual needs, and trying to change things that we can't really change is counterproductive and depressing. Weigh up the things you do that make a difference, and you'll probably be surprised at how much you already do. Join a group or organisation that can help support others, or raise awareness of the problems our planet is facing. Carry on with your good habits, like recycling what you can, and remember that every item recycled is less resources that have to be mined or drilled for, which has the knock on effect of conserving water and protecting our waterways.

It's also worth remembering that while we as individuals have the power to make small changes, the biggest changes have to happen from the top down. We need people in power, or with money, that want to stop deforestation; that want to protect indigenous peoples who strive every day of their lives to conserve the natural environments they live in; who understand that intensive farming has long term impacts that we need to consider; who grasp the importance of ancient woodlands and how vital trees are for flood defences, habitats, and even human mental health. You might have a week where you're not able to recycle or had to use the car every day, but of you were able to sign a petition, or write to your elected official or even share a post on social media raising awareness of these issues, then you are fighting the good fight; the fight to save our planet before it's too late.

I'm not suggesting that Pagans are the only people who can make a difference in this world. Everyone can make a difference. Absolutely everyone. But, as I see Pagan communities strengthening their ties, speaking out loud about their love of nature and our planet, being kinder to themselves and others, I wonder if Paganism could at the very least be a catalytic force in the movement towards a more compassionate way of living. Let's try, at least. Let's keep talking about why the world *needs* us to step up. Humans have made a bit of a mess of this beautiful planet, but they can absolutely do plenty to help fix it too. Let your conscience and your spirituality drive you even further to be the change you want to see. Let your spirituality give you the resilience to persevere with the work that needs to be done.

Resources

Finding ways to connect your own path to your desire to help the planet will no doubt be a deeply personal journey. This subchapter provides ideas intended to be inspiration, rather than things for you to carbon-copy into your own spirituality. Of course, if any of these ideas speaks to you, use them to your heart's content!

Eco-Friendly Offering Ideas

Some of these are deities which you may have honoured or worked with, but others you may be less familiar with. Of course, there are thousands of deities throughout modern spirituality, so this is just a very small selection. For each deity, I've included offerings that are kinder to the environment whilst still being generally favoured by this particular form of divinity. I hope that these examples give you some ideas, but please go with what your heart, mind, spirit, or deity tells you.

Aphrodite – roses, particularly rose petals that you have grown or responsibly foraged.

Apollo – sing for him or write a piece of poetry.

Brigid – also appreciates poetry, but a physical offering could include oats, oatcakes, or milk.

Cailleach – coins which you can cleanse and use again, or leave on the altar – never ones that you will spend; snow or plain water; seaweed.

Cave Spirits – if spirits are unnamed and generic, learn a little about the place they reside at. Rocks commonly found here could be discovered and left, or a little pile of native earth, or a plant that grows near the cave. Never take too much and be mindful not to disrupt the ecosystem.

Cernunnos – an elusive god associated with European continental

Celts but also adopted by some neo-pagan religions as their Horned God. Biodegradable offerings include milk, moss, animal horns (ethically sourced), or leaves from local trees.

Cerridwen – small pieces of meat like pork, if appropriate; coffee, or wheat.

The Dagda – oats or porridge, a cauldron of home grown treats, clean water, music, especially from a harp or other stringed instrument; roast meat, if appropriate.

Freya – honey or mead, remembering to use only small amounts of alcohol to avoid ecological damage; cider or apple juice; poetry, particularly that on themes of love.

Frigga – pieces of birch including leaves, catkins or bark; handspun yarn, which is a great way to combine learning a skill with honouring your deity; milk.

The Green Man – the Green Man is something more of a concept that one specific deity. The Green Man and his instantly recognisable face spewing leaves almost uncontrollably is so visceral and familiar; a spirit of nature, the heart of the forest who needs no naming. Indeed, the name "man" is almost misleading, as this complex spirit embodies all nature, hardly just the male-presenting parts. Considering honouring this green and vital being with commitments to plant trees, compost, use less energy, or simply walk among the woods with an open mind and heart.

Hekate – my Great Lady of the twin torches who holds the keys to the mysteries. Consider offerings of almonds, garlic and olive oil, which are all received well and easily disposed of. Don't compost Hekate's offerings; lay them at a crossroads at the Dark Moon. You may eat a portion of whatever you offer, but keep Hers on a separate plate or in a separate area. Don't look back as you walk away from the crossroads.

Herne – often spoken of as a counterpart to Cernunnos or other Horned God archetypes, but is, in fact, a local legend centred around Berkshire in England. Herne is a phantom hunter, made famous by William Shakespeare in his play, *The Merry Wives of Windsor*. Herne is a manifestation of the Wild Hunt, a common myth throughout various forms of folklore. Honour the hunt with food from your table, left outside with your doors closed.

House Spirits – these are many and varied, so always research your local area's folklore and traditions before settling on your preferred offerings. Some local to me like butter or cream. Others, like the Norwegian Nisse, need porridge with a pat of butter on top. Research is everything.

Loki – cinnamon and other "warm" spices; sweet foods such as candy and candy apples; chilli peppers.

Lugh – a deity I am particularly fond of, and over the years I have found him most interested in seasonal fruits, particularly the berries I forage during my summer excursions. Lugh is also a many-skilled god, so honour him by committing to learn a new skill, improving an existing skill, or by presenting something you created yourself. This could even be a song or a poem, as he was a master musician and *filí,* a type of poet working in words of satire and power.

The Mórrígan – *An Mórrígan*, Great Queen, Phantom Queen; whatever you call Her, she is appreciative of service, good whiskey, and heartfelt words. In our house, She receives apples, a splash of wine, treasures from my foraging trips, and hard work.

Odin – crow or raven feathers if ethically sourced; ash leaves; the crafting of or working with runes.

Rhiannon – horse hair if ethically sourced; images of horses; white flowers, thinking about what is local to you; feathers.

River Spirits – send a charm into the river made of small pieces of locally scavenged wood, leaves, and feathers.

Seashore or Coastal Spirits – shells, seaweed, driftwood, tiny amounts of salt, and music that echoes the sounds of the sea.

Fresh Water Spirits – water spirits are diverse across the world, so research what resides locally and act accordingly. For example, the spirit of a still and dark green pond will be very different to the spirit of a crystal clear lake that stretches for miles. Keep your offerings local, and never commit anything you're not truly prepared to give; remember, water is both violent and destructive when riled.

Taliesin – Taliesin is technically not a deity, but is still revered to the point of worship by some. This bard or poet may be offered words of your own, a commitment to learn a long tale or story of your ancestors, or music.

Thor – food from your meal, particularly if it contains onions, garlic, or meat; images of goats, carts, weapons; beer.

Woodland Spirits – seeds or leaves from local trees, preferably found on the ground and never too much.

Voluntary work to improve the local area or raise awareness of conservation issues.

Useful Correspondences

We saw a bee en route today
Round and hungry, charged with sunlight.
Charged round town did we, then paused to play
Amidst the song of feathered flight.

The following are a few animals, elements, and even seasons that can be linked to environmental themes. These ones are close to me, on my personal path.

Action: Create a list of important symbols or images from your own path and see if and how they connect to the health of the planet or environment.

Bees – community, hard work, many small actions making a big change.

Ants – similar to bees, but they also remind us of how things might seem unchanged on the surface yet may be changing dramatically in unseen ways. Just peer inside any ants' nest if you ever get the opportunity. The completely transform the land they take over – very like humans.

Spiders – industry, perseverance, and belief in one's self. Watch a spider make a web over and over as it gets battered by passing birds or the wind. Can we keep fixing things, in the face of such destruction? I hope so.

Crows – crows clean up after us, over and over. They take away parts of corpses, rotten food, and are the unseen janitors of our towns and cities. Imagine what life might be like without our scavenging corvid friends.

Cats – cats are the most self-sufficient of our pets, yet they are still full of love and affection. Something to aspire to, perhaps.

Earth – honouring the Earth is the core tenet of this book. We all honour Her in different ways, and hopefully you now have a few more ways to try and do just that.

Air – air blows around us as the wind, it fills our lungs with life, and it refreshes and rejuvenates. It reminds us of the carefree attitudes of childhood, reminding us to be open to new ideas and to look at this world with the wonder that makes us want to protect it, now more than ever.

Fire – fire is both warming and gentle yet harsh and destructive. Like human nature, it can crush or rebuild, depending upon how it is used. Let us channel our fires in the right way.

Water – like fire, water gives life and destroys. Water is also linked to emotion and dreams, helping us channel our love for this planet into hopes for the future that we have to bring to fruition.

Apples – apples are a symbol of youth, vitality, immortality, and healing. I leave offerings of apples to the Irish deities I honour, as a symbol of undying devotion and my commitment to other living things.

Blackberries – blackberries are a very seasonal fruit where I live, and remind me of the turn of the seasons. Over the past few years, I have also been using them as a barometer to measure climate change; the flowers stay a little later every year.

Spring – spring is the start of things; new life, eggs, melting snows. It reminds us that everything needs a first step and that large tasks are accomplished by the smallest of actions.

Summer – summer is a season of heat and joy, but more recently of storms and flooding, or great droughts. Summer teaches us to take notice of the changing world, and stay true to our commitments to make changes in positive ways.

Autumn or Fall – autumn is, for me, the most transitional of seasons. The colourful leaves and migrating birds remind us that change is always possible.

Winter – as deciduous plants die back and certain mammals start to hibernate, winter is a reminder that it is always okay to rest and take stock; to reflect upon our achievements so far and what we want for the future. We don't always have to be *doing*.

Moon – the moon is so far away, so separate, yet this stunning satellite affects the whole planet in gargantuan ways. The moon is so prominent in so many faiths, and in so many different ways, but we can all surely agree that the Moon symbolises the power even a single person can have to make the most profound and lasting change.

Sun – the sun is a symbol of power, sometimes growing, sometimes fading, but always there and ever-present. May we never forget the power we all hold, as individuals *and* as communities.

Uses of Common Ingredients

In Chapter 5 I gave you a list of commonly available ingredients to use in incense. You can also use these ingredients as offerings, in poppets, pouches, or simply as tools for meditation. Here is that list again but including what you might use them for.

Rosemary – enhanced memory and revisiting forgotten memories, cleansing an area, and protection.

Rose flowers – deepened emotions, confidence, and a sense of calm.

Lavender – strongly linked to sleep and relaxation, plus can help balance the emotions.

Asafoetida (small amounts) – linked to Saturn, breaking shackles and boundaries, repelling evil and breaking hexes and curses.

Cinnamon (small amounts, perhaps better for outdoor burning as cinnamon smoke can irritate some people) – attraction of positive energy, associations with fire and fire beings, and linked to passion and creativity.

Pine resin which you can often find on the trunks of pine trees and peel off like glue – one of the oldest forms of incense, used for many different reasons including purification or exorcism, which may simply mean banishing negative energy. If you buy it, you may see it labelled as colophony.

Sage (culinary or home-grown; I don't advocate sourcing exotic strains of sage as they're not always sustainable or culturally appropriate) – cleansing, purification, and may help bring the answer to complex problems by clearing your mind as well as your physical space.

Allspice powder or berries – to attract wealth and good luck.

Juniper berries – psychic and physical protection, and for purification of an area.

Citrus fruit peel like lime, lemon or orange – generally associated with the sun, fire, love, divination, and money.

Dried apple – brings a sense of refreshment, associated with healing and immortality.

Chamomile – calming and relaxing, helps those who struggle to sleep.

Various tree bark – we often find strips of bark on the ground where squirrels have been feeding, so figuring out what type of bark it is can be the first step! Birch bark is associated with magical flight, courage, and protection. Oak can be used in abundance magic. Never burn the bark of an elder tree; they are considered protected in many faiths, and there are many different tales of ill luck or even death following anyone who would intentionally harm an elder tree.

Magical Fruit and Veg

Growing vegetables is good for you and the planet, but can also be a magical experience. Here are some brief correspondences to get you started; do research your favourites and explore the folklore and mythology associated with plants. It can be truly fascinating.

Carrots: Fertility
Olives: Protection from lightening
Beans: Healing warts
Beets: Love magic, magical ink
Çelery: Increased psychic ability
Peas: Wealth, healing warts
Onions: Absorb negativity
Potatoes: To make poppets (Gives a whole new meaning to Mr Potato Head, right?)
Tomatoes: Protects against evil
Sweetcorn: Luck, love and the power of the smallest things

Pagan Environmentalism Glossary

Air Pollution: Toxic chemicals and gases introduced to the air, either indoors or outdoors, usually due to human activity.
Atmosphere: All the air between us and space.
Biodegradable: If something is biodegradable, it can be broken down by living organisms.
Carbon Dioxide: CO2, gas produced naturally by living things

and removed naturally by plants and bodies of water. Fossil fuels have increased the natural amount of CO_2 in the atmosphere, which may be contributing to global warming, particularly as the natural carbon sinks like forests are being depleted.

Carbon footprint: A measure of how much carbon we produce in our daily lives, giving an idea of the impact of our activities on the environment and climate change.

Carbon neutral: A term used for activities which absorb as much CO_2 as they produce. For example, the motorsport Formula 1 aims to be completely carbon neutral by 2030, despite generating huge amounts of carbon both on track and when travelling between races. They aim to do this by increasing the recycling of waste, eliminating single use items, and using biofuels as well as electricity to power the cars. This is known as *carbon offsetting*, whereby an organisation takes action to positively counter the negative impact they are having on the environment.

Energy efficient: Using the least amount of energy for the maximum output. For example, replacing incandescent lightbulbs with LED lightbulbs, as incandescent bulbs waste much of their energy as heat.

Global warming: The increase in the Earth's average temperature due to human overproduction of gases like carbon dioxide.

Landfill: Massive holes filled with a mixture or refuse (waste) that biodegrades at vastly varying rates.

Litter: Anything discarded by humans in a place it shouldn't be.

Off-grid: Living without reliance on public utilities; sourcing one's own water and power or the water and power for a whole community.

Offerings: Anything given in honour or worship to a deity, spirit, or otherworldly being. Offerings can be physical or intangible, such as songs, poetry, or prayer. Offerings can also consist of your time, effort, or devotion to a worthy cause.

Organic: Anything living or once living. Organic offerings, for example, are ones made from plants or animals in some way. This could range from a bowl of seeds to a small collection of scavenged bones.

Paganism: A collection of religions, faiths, and spiritual paths which are generally associated with polytheism, although not exclusively, and also generally linked to a reverence for nature and an understanding of the equality of genders. Many varieties of Paganism exist and some exist even outside these very approximate guidelines.

Recycle: Returning waste to a facility where it can be broken down into key components which are then used to make other products. This conserves natural resources.

Reduce: Using and buying less products, in an effort to conserve natural resources.

Re-use: Reusing products instead of throwing them away, either by repurposing them or upcycling them into something new.

Ritual: Any task or process that you repeat over and over in the same or similar fashion each time. Sacred ritual normally follows a particular set of guidelines or steps each time, although other factors may change to make each ritual pertinent to the specific reason it is being performed.

Self-sufficient: Able to survive purely on the efforts on one's own hard work, for example growing or raising food, living off-grid, or crafting one's own tools. Self-sufficiency can be a journey, for example, you might make certain things yourself or grow a portion of your own food.

Spiritual: Anything connected to the spirit or soul; being spiritual is a level of concern for that part of you which is connected to something larger or other than human, possibly called divinity but equally known as universal energy or the spirit.

Sustainable: Something that is viable long-term; resources that can be renewed; energy that does not deplete resources; development that does not reduce the ability of future generations to continue their own development.

Upcycle: Transforming something which is no longer useful or wanted in its current form into something which is useful or desirable in some way.

Worship: Reverence or adoration for something outside oneself. This may be directed at a deity or deities, a spirit, the spirits of many things, or a concept such as nature, or the anthropomorphising of a non-human entity, such as the concept of Mother Earth or Father Sky.

Further Reading

How to Save the Planet by Luke Eastwood

Practically Pagan: An Alternative Guide to Cooking by Rachel Patterson

Pagan Portals: Poppets and Magical Dolls by Lucya Starza

Every Day Magic, Edited by Lucya Starza

Useful Links

https://abcbirds.org/

https://www.rspb.org.uk/

https://www.woodlandtrust.org.uk/

https://environmentjournal.online/articles/is-there-any-point-in-recycling/

https://www.recycleacrossamerica.org/recycling-facts

http://nda.ie/Resources/Accessibility-toolkit/Make-your-buildings-more-accessible/

https://www.worldwildlife.org/industries/soy

https://assets.publishing.service.gov.uk/government/uploads/system/uploads/attachment_data/file/897289/countryside-code-leaflet.pdf

https://www.asthma.org.uk/advice/triggers/pollution/

https://uk-air.defra.gov.uk/air-pollution/daqi

http://www.bbc.co.uk/gardening/today_in_your_garden/community_projects.shtml

https://www.nsalg.org.uk/about-us/vacancies/
https://www.farmgarden.org.uk/clas
https://thecommunitysgarden.com/
https://www.greenpeace.org.uk/
https://responsiblesoy.org/?lang=en
https://www.epa.gov/ghgemissions/sources-greenhouse-gas-emissions
https://www.pfcommunity.org.uk/aether-patches/
https://climate.nasa.gov/effects/
https://www.roadmaptozero.com/landingpage/chemcheck
https://www.bbc.co.uk/sport/formula1/50382898
https://folklorethursday.com/
https://irishpaganschool.com/

Sources

Current Biology: The Iceman's Last Meal Consisted of Fat, Wild Meat, and Cereals (Volume 28, Issue 14); Frank Maixner et al, 2018.

The Department for Environment, Food and Rural Affairs (DEFRA)

Environment Journal Online, articles including "Is there any point in recycling?", Katy Wheeler, 2019.

Dieter, C.A., Maupin, M.A., Caldwell, R.R., Harris, M.A., Ivahnenko, T.I., Lovelace, J.K., Barber, N.L., and Linsey, K.S., 2018, Estimated use of water in the United States in 2015: U.S. Geological Survey Circular 1441, 65 p., https://doi.org/10.3133/cir1441

The Story of Soy; WWF, 2016.

Interaction with indoor plants may reduce psychological and physiological stress by suppressing autonomic nervous system activity in young adults: a randomized crossover study; Min-Sun Lee, Juyoung Lee, Bum-Jin Park, Yoshifumi Mayazaki; The Journal of Physical Anthropology, 2015.

Are E-Readers Greener Than Books?, Joe Hutsko, New York Times, 2009.

Are crystals the new blood diamonds? Eva Wiseman, The Guardian, 2019.

Turn Around Deforestation in 2020; António Guterres, United Nations, March 2020.

Meet the Indigenous community that's fighting deforestation – and winning; Helle Abelvik-Lawson, Greenpeace, November 2020.

British chicken driving deforestation in Brazil's "second Amazon"; Alexandra Heal, Andrew Wasley, Emma Howard, Alice Ross, Lucy Jordan, Harry Holmes; The Bureau of Investigative Journalism, November 2020.

Sources of Greenhouse Gas Emissions; United States Environmental Protection Agency, 2018.

The Next New Species Could be in Your Backyard: Why Exploration and Discovery Matter – Everywhere; Gregory M. Mueller, Ph.D., National Geographic, 2014.

The Effects of Climate Change; NASA, 2020.

Dynamic ice loss from the Greenland Ice Sheet driven by sustained glacier retreat; Michalea D. King, Ian M. Howat, Salvatore G. Candela, Myoung J. Noh, Seongsu Jeong, Brice P. Y. Noël, Michiel R. van den Broeke, Bert Wouters, and Adelaide Negrete; Communications Earth & Environment, August 2020.

Extinction Rebellion Doorstep David Attenborough; Elisa Menendez, The Metro, 2020.

Eco-activists injured in 20-foot drop from trees when contractors cut their ropes; Sam Courtney-Guy, The Metro, 2020.

Internet Usage Statistics (IWS), World Internet Users and 2020 Population Stats; Miniwatts Marketing Group, 2020.

Tens of thousands of trees die as HS2 bosses say replacing them more 'cost-effective' than watering; Jon Sharman, The Independent, 2019.

Other Books in the *Practically Pagan* series you may enjoy...

Cooking
...no fuss cooking to nourish the body, spirit and soul
Rachel Patterson
978-1-78904-379-2 (Paperback)
978-1-78904-380-8 (e-book)

Gardening
...live in a way that helps the planet
Elen Sentier
978-1-78904-373-0 (Paperback)
978-1-78904-374-7 (e-book)

Magical Living
...natural spirituality, and all things witchy
Maria DeBlassie
978-1-78904-403-4 (Paperback)
978-1-78904-404-1 (e-book)

Health & Well-being
...a gift and a sacred prayer of intention
Irisanya Moon

978-1-78904-377-8 (Paperback)
978-1-78904-378-5 (e-book)

**MOON
BOOKS**

PAGANISM & SHAMANISM

What is Paganism? A religion, a spirituality, an alternative belief system, nature worship? You can find support for all these definitions (and many more) in dictionaries, encyclopaedias, and text books of religion, but subscribe to any one and the truth will evade you. Above all Paganism is a creative pursuit, an encounter with reality, an exploration of meaning and an expression of the soul. Druids, Heathens, Wiccans and others, all contribute their insights and literary riches to the Pagan tradition. Moon Books invites you to begin or to deepen your own encounter, right here, right now.

If you have enjoyed this book, why not tell other readers by posting a review on your preferred book site.

Recent bestsellers from Moon Books are:

Journey to the Dark Goddess
How to Return to Your Soul
Jane Meredith
Discover the powerful secrets of the Dark Goddess and
transform your depression, grief and pain into healing
and integration.
Paperback: 978-1-84694-677-6 ebook: 978-1-78099-223-5

Shamanic Reiki
Expanded Ways of Working with Universal Life Force Energy
Llyn Roberts, Robert Levy
Shamanism and Reiki are each powerful ways of healing; together,
their power multiplies. *Shamanic Reiki* introduces techniques to
help healers and Reiki practitioners tap ancient healing wisdom.
Paperback: 978-1-84694-037-8 ebook: 978-1-84694-650-9

Pagan Portals – The Awen Alone
Walking the Path of the Solitary Druid
Joanna van der Hoeven
An introductory guide for the solitary Druid, *The Awen Alone* will
accompany you as you explore, and seek out your own place
within the natural world.
Paperback: 978-1-78279-547-6 ebook: 978-1-78279-546-9

A Kitchen Witch's World of Magical Herbs & Plants
Rachel Patterson
A journey into the magical world of herbs and plants, filled with
magical uses, folklore, history and practical magic. By popular
writer, blogger and kitchen witch, Tansy Firedragon.
Paperback: 978-1-78279-621-3 ebook: 978-1-78279-620-6

Medicine for the Soul
The Complete Book of Shamanic Healing
Ross Heaven
All you will ever need to know about shamanic healing and how to
become your own shaman...
Paperback: 978-1-78099-419-2 ebook: 978-1-78099-420-8

Shaman Pathways – The Druid Shaman
Exploring the Celtic Otherworld
Danu Forest
A practical guide to Celtic shamanism with exercises and
techniques as well as traditional lore for exploring the Celtic
Otherworld.
Paperback: 978-1-78099-615-8 ebook: 978-1-78099-616-5

Readers of ebooks can buy or view any of these bestsellers by
clicking on the live link in the title. Most titles are published in
paperback and as an ebook. Paperbacks are available in traditional
bookshops. Both print and ebook formats are available online.

Find more titles and sign up to our readers' newsletter at
http://www.johnhuntpublishing.com/paganism
Follow us on Facebook at https://www.facebook.com/MoonBooks
and Twitter at https://twitter.com/MoonBooksJHP